CLASSIC
SAIL

CLASSIC SAIL

Joseph Gribbins

MetroBooks

MetroBooks

An Imprint of Friedman/Fairfax Publishers

©2001, 1998 by Michael Friedman Publishing Group, Inc.

Library of Congress Cataloging-in-Publication Data available upon request.

ISBN 1-58663-312-0

Editor: Ann Kirby-Payne
Art Director: Jeff Batzli
Designer: Maria M. Mann
Photography Editor: Wendy Missan
Production Manager: Jeanne E. Hunter

Color separations by Colourscan Overseas Co. Pte. Ltd.
Printed in China by Leefung-Asco Printers Ltd.

10 9 8 7 6 5 4 3 2 1

For bulk purchases and special sales, please contact:
Friedman/Fairfax Publishers
Attention: Sales Department
230 Fifth Avenue
New York, NY 10001
212/685-6610   FAX 212/685-3916

Visit our website:
www.metrobooks.com

Contents

Introduction..........8

Chapter One

Ancient Sail..........14

Chapter Two

Nineteenth-Century Sail..........28

Chapter Three

Day Boats..........46

Chapter Four

Cruising Classics..........62

Chapter Five

Racing Classics..........78

Chapter Six

Replicas and Reinterpretations..........92

Chapter Seven

Luxury Yachts..........108

Sources..........124

Index..........127

Introduction

Driving an automobile is a twentieth-century experience. Riding a horse or driving a team of them can be understood as a nineteenth-century experience, even though riding and coaching are far older human modes of transportation and sport. Sailing a boat is a very old experience—the thrill of tiller vibrating and sail pulling aboard a modern fiberglass day boat is very much the same today as what a Roman waterman would have experienced aboard a husky little spritsail boat two thousand years ago.

That ancient connection, along with the simple technology of managing the sailor's bag of wind, may be part of sailing's timeless appeal. A sailboat represents relatively low technology—strong sticks, strong ropes, cloth contrived in various shapes—compared with, say, a windmill or a locomotive. But it can be highly sophisticated in structure and in use, with sails and spars crafted to be light and strong at the same time, individual sails and rigs designed to do a variety of nimble things, and sail arrangements specially suited to the weather and the course. A sailor must read the wind and the waves while a cruise progresses, making constant decisions and adjustments to keep the boat moving efficiently and safely along. More than most human activities, sailing makes demands on the practitioner's wit and experience, and this is certainly one of its attractions. Unlike most forms of powerboating, sailing is active and involving, and sailors like it that way. Even a relaxing sunset sail down the harbor and back will involve sail-handling, an eye on the weather, a few tacks and jibes, and the hope that the evening breeze doesn't fade before the sailor gets home.

There are types of sailboats, types of sailors, and types of sailing. Casual sailors—proprietors of summer cottages that happen to have a sailboat on the waterfront, power-boaters who keep a sailing dinghy on the boat deck—do it for the diversion it affords.

The restored 109-foot (33.2m) schooner *Mariette,* a classic designed and built by Nat Herreshoff in 1916, pegs the speedo under full sail.

Racing sailors—in a spectrum that ranges from one-design competitors on inland lakes to athletes aboard million-dollar yachts racing around the world—do it for the excitement and challenge it generates. Cruising sailors—from weekenders sailing to an offshore island for a nautical camping trip to people who wander the world's oceans in boats that are also their homes—do it for the escape it promises. The truth is that sailing can deliver a welcome diversion, elevated adrenalin, and an escape from boring routine to all sailors.

We consider classic sailboats in this book—sailboats that are mostly wood and canvas rather than fiberglass and carbon fiber. These sailing classics are the recent ancestors of sailboats that have been made from newer materials since the 1960s. They are as ancient as Polynesian voyaging canoes and as modern as the great J-boats. They are classic because they are excellent and enduring designs, and most of them are undeniably beautiful.

We consider sailing and sailing machines from a historical perspective that reveals the technology of the thing as ancient and basic, and explores its use and influence in seafaring cultures around the world. We look at the nineteenth century as a technical and historical zenith of commercial sail and the real beginning of sailing as sport and recreation. And we look at some classic sailboats in familiar categories—daysailing, racing, cruising, re-creating the sailing past.

Are classic (that is, older) sailboats better than the newer creations of plastic and aluminum, stainless steel, and carbon fiber—fast catamarans and trimarans for voyagers, Whitbread 60s, Lasers, Hobie Cats, modern racing sloops that in recent years have beaten clipper-ship sailing records around Cape Horn from New York to San Francisco?

No, the older, classic sailboats are not necessarily better—often, they are not even prettier. Some of these new boats are stunning combinations of space-age materials and stark, functional shapes. But classic sailboats are familiar and beloved and beautiful—even the new sailors of the 1990s admire them. We invite you to admire them, too, in the pages of this book.

PREVIOUS PAGES: International One-Designs sail at Northeast Harbor, Maine. RIGHT: *Creole* combines luxury with sail-carrying power.

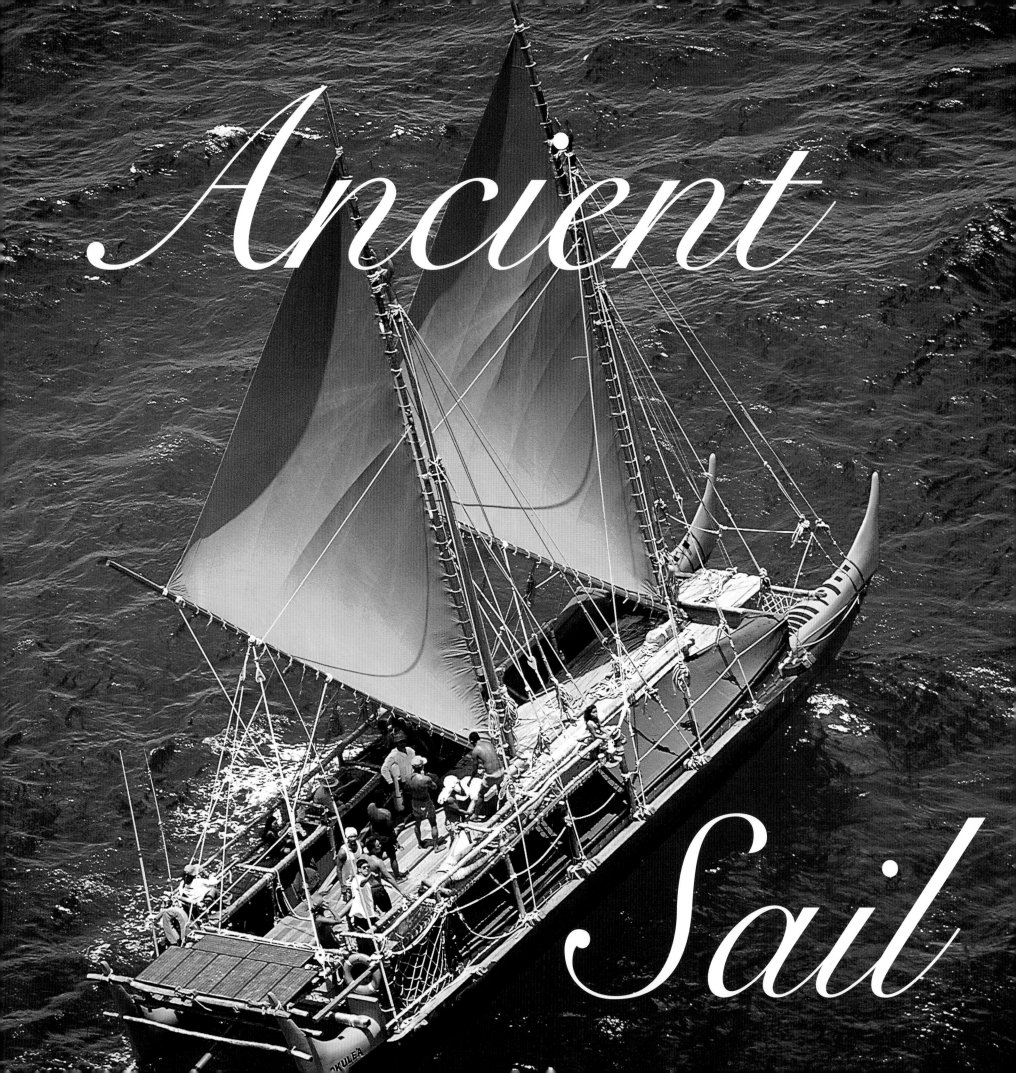

Chapter One

THE OLDEST KNOWN IMAGE OF A SHIP WITH A SAIL DECORATES AN EGYPTIAN FUNERARY VASE THAT DATES TO ROUGHLY 5000 B.C. WE HAVE NO ARCHAEOLOGICAL OR PICTORIAL EVIDENCE FOR ANY EARLIER APPEARANCE OF SAILS MADE FROM LEATHER OR WOVEN MATS OR CRUDE CLOTH, OR EVEN BRANCHES FULL OF LEAVES HELD UP TO

catch the wind. But the wind was there, and it must have been compelling. There can be no doubt that the nautical adventurers of the Bronze Age, and maybe even the Stone Age, felt the power of the wind on their bodies and on their vessels as they foraged the shoreline or struggled home in a dugout canoe through a storm.

At what point such people made the connection between that power and the forward motion that might be had from a bag of wind is lost to us. The Egyptians left records of nearly everything they did and believed; their predecessors in Asia, Africa, the Americas, and Europe generally did not. But modern archaeology is increasingly able to trace migrations of people across land and water, and there were plenty of migrations more than seven thousand years ago. Some of them would have been made under sail.

The settlement of Australia from Southeast Asia is now thought to have happened at least sixty thousand years ago—taking people across a forty-mile (64km) stretch of water between Bali and an island called Lombok in the chain of Indonesian islands that trends east to Australia. There was never a convenient land bridge there, so seagoing humans had to go over in some form of vessel. British naturalist Alfred Russel Wallace in the 1860s described this stretch of water as an absolute biological barrier, and noted that tigers never crossed it to populate Australia and that kangaroos never crossed it to populate Asia. But clever humans did.

The replica Polynesian voyaging canoe *Hokule'a* sails serenely downwind with two triangular sails. *Hokule'a* made a replica voyage from Hawaii to Tahiti and back in 1976.

Other clever humans are believed to have populated most of island-studded Southeast Asia more than forty thousand years ago. Whoever they were, they seem to have decided to settle their abundant seacoast and not move down the chain of islands to Australia. The Pacific coast of South America has recently been proposed as a landfall for seafaring people as much as thirty thousand years ago. There is some evidence for this in Chile, and it remains a mystery whether people arrived there by sea or came with a very early migration across the ice of the Bering Strait and down the length of both Americas. They may have come from two directions.

More than ten thousand years ago, seafarers were active in the Aegean, where obsidian—the volcanic glass that furnished sharp tools and weapons—was obtained by enterprising mainlanders from offshore islands. Log rafts are thought to have been the vessels these people paddled to the islands and back. Bamboo rafts are suggested as the vehicles that took people from Asia to Australia and perhaps to the islands and coasts of Southeast Asia.

Sometime in the fifty thousand–odd years between that earliest sea migration from Asia to Australia and the picture of a vessel with a sail on an Egyptian vase, the now-sophisticated technology of sailing began. It probably began with a square sail—a small, simple surface aloft for the wind to push—and must have been accompanied by the rudiments of sparring and rigging. It must have amazed early sailors how powerful their little bag of wind could be—just as it amazes small-boat sailors today. At first their sails must have flailed away from them and broken the ropes and sticks contrived to keep the rig under control. Trial and error sorted things out eventually, and experimentation commenced just as soon as skills developed to manage such sailing arrangements as a raft with a square sail on a bipod mast or a canoe with a leafy branch stuck up in the air.

The experimenters then became sailors. And sailors, true to their origins perhaps, are always experimenters. The process of refining the technology and the skills of the thing must have progressed through ages of sail-powered vehicles of a variety of types—dugout canoes, boats made from bundled reeds, rafts of wood or bamboo, boats made of animal hide stitched around a wood frame, and canoes and larger vessels built from thin wood sewn or fitted or pegged together. The sail, like the wheel, seems to have appeared in many places all over the world with no record of or even guess about its origins and migrations. It was a good idea that must have occurred to many people in many places. It was power to be managed—a thing that attracts all humans.

The square sail persisted a long time in sailing technology, from the earliest records of its use in Egypt, Phoenicia, and the Greece of Homer to the end of the nineteenth century, when square-rigged barks still carried cargo around the world and Norwegian fishermen went north under square sail to a cod fishery above the Arctic Circle. The open boats of the Norwegian fishermen were almost the same as the Viking ships of their ancestors.

As much as six thousand years ago, bigger square sails and vessels to match widened the horizons of seafaring and shipbuilding people. Daysails to and from nearby fishing grounds, or local modes of transport—Egyptian trips up the Nile under sail to the quarries, for example, and trips back with a heavy load of stone pushed downstream by the current—in time gave way to real voyaging, and this presupposes sailing. Galleys, large vessels with teams of rowers, were useful in war or for short passages, but sail was more energy-efficient since the wind was free. Egyptian sailing ships are known to have raided the coast of Syria fifty-four hundred years ago, and more than five thousand years ago the Egyptians were trading with African ports in the Red Sea and with Lebanese ports in the eastern Mediterranean. Egyptian sailing ships were so big by the time of Queen Hatshepsut—thirty-five hundred years ago—that one of the vessels on record was able to carry two three-hundred-ton (272t) stone obelisks, each about one hundred feet (30m) long.

In the Pacific, migrations into an ocean world of islands larger than the landmass of Europe and Asia combined are thought to have begun fifty-five hundred years ago, necessarily in sailing canoes and in catamarans made from two canoes fixed together with a bridge in between. These sailors eventually settled Hawaii and New Zealand, and may have reached Easter Island and the mainland of South America.

The Phoenicians of what are now the coasts of Lebanon and Israel succeeded the Egyptians as the great traders and voyagers of the West, and by twenty-eight hundred years ago began to establish colonies and trading stations all over the Mediterranean. The Greek historian Herodotus reported that Phoenicians managed to circumnavigate Africa twenty-six hundred years ago by sailing south from

The inside of a classical Greek drinking cup shows us a Greek ship with squaresail and steering oar. Appropriately, its occupant is Dionysius.

Roman ships carved into a marble sarcophagus sail downwind under squaresail with anxious sailors tending sails and steering gear. A man has gone overboard.

Suez and always keeping land to the right. It took four years for these sailors to return to the Mediterranean through the Straits of Gibraltar. This may or may not have happened; if it did, more than two thousand years would pass before Portuguese navigators were able to repeat the feat in reverse, sailing south along the Atlantic coast. The Phoenicians were capable of such long-legged sailing. Distant voyages from Phoenician bases in the Mediterranean are part of the record of ancient seafaring—down the west coast of Africa, to primitive ports in western Europe, and to Cornwall in England.

THE EVOLUTION OF SAIL TYPES

Commerce under sail was common in the Mediterranean three thousand years ago among the Egyptians, Phoenicians, Canaanites, Cretans, and mainland Greeks. As coastal and deep-water voyaging grew, the technology of sailing evolved to larger and more manageable sails, and even to the great secret of progress under sail—moving not only with the wind's strong push but with its pull, with the wind ahead of the boat. How a sailboat could move into the wind was a mystery until the twentieth century, even though sailors had been refining sails and rigging to do it better since the Greece of Homer.

In 1738 the Swiss physicist Daniel Bernoulli explained the dynamics of fluids in this way: for any moving fluid, pressure plus speed is a constant; if a fluid moves faster, pressure is reduced; and if a fluid moves slower, pressure is increased. Bernoulli's law applies to gases, too, and in the case of an airplane wing, with air moving at uneven speeds over the flat bottom and the curved top, there is a pressure difference that pulls the wing up. This is what happens to a curved sail slicing into the wind, but until the airplane wing was invented and the principles of flight became clear, no sailor in the world understood what was happening.

A square sail full of wind can be an airfoil. As its angle into the wind increases, its pulling power grows stronger until, like a wing, it comes too much into the wind and stalls or luffs with nearly equal pressure on both sides. Early sailors noticed these things and made use of them in developing sails and sailing vessels that could move whether the wind was ahead, astern, or from the side. Nonetheless, most voyages under sail, from the time of Queen Hatshepsut through Europe's Middle Ages, were made with prevailing winds that sailors knew—local breezes that sprang up in the afternoon, Red Sea winds that blew one way for half the year and then reversed direction, mid-Pacific winds that always blew from west to east. And voyages that used these winds were nearly always made with the wind behind, pushing the sails. Sailing before the wind was easier, more predictable, and much less demanding for sail-handling crew. One reason that Columbus was able to cross the Atlantic and come back again was that he knew from long experience—voyaging north to England and Scandinavia and south to the bulge of West Africa—that his ships would be blown steadily west by the winds he would find below Gibraltar and would be blown back to Europe by the winds he would find farther north.

The Romans added a small square sail at the bow of each of their very large ships. Cocked at various angles to the wind, this helped them to maneuver in close quarters and to steer a straight course at sea. At the same time, and probably even before, small vessels were fitted with a simple spritsail, a square-shaped sail with a pole run diagonally up to one of its corners. This could function as a square-before-the-wind sail or as an airfoil that drew the boat into the wind. It was the spritsail that likely developed the sailor's art of tacking: sailing into the wind by having the force of the wind on one side of the sail or the other, then changing sides when forward motion or maneuvering room diminished—sailing a zigzag course into the wind.

The Arabs developed the lateen sail after the time of the Romans and the Greeks, and whether they appreciated it or not they developed a sailing airfoil. The lateen sail—a big triangle of cloth that can be presented to the wind in a variety of ways—has powered the vessels of the Indian Ocean, the Red Sea, the Persian Gulf, and some other trading areas of the Muslim world for well over a thousand years. It is a simple device, a long triangular sail that hangs from a yard attached nearly at the top of a short mast, and can be cocked high in the air to catch a breeze. The lateen rig can be hard to manage in a blow, and to tack it, one must steer the vessel in a nearly 360-degree turn. The lateen sail has migrated far from the Persian Gulf (where it is thought to have originated) as the only sail on many vessels from the Arab world, as the aftermost (mizzen) sail on the ships of Columbus and on many local vessels of the Mediterranean, and

A fleet of the Ottoman powers that threatened Europe in the sixteenth century blockades Marseilles. All have winglike lateen sails invented and spread throughout the Muslim world by Arab sailors.

as the sail favored by Italian fishermen not only in Europe but a hundred years ago in San Francisco. In modified form it appears on the familiar Sunfish sport sailboat.

South Sea island sailors developed triangular and claw-shaped sails that operated on principles similar to those of the lateen rig. Their voyages in single canoes, double canoes (catamarans), and outriggers (canoes with a small balancing hull attached) were made with one or two sails on simple spars that could be maneuvered to accommodate the wind from behind, to the side, and to some extent forward. More than anything else, it was Polynesian navigation techniques—sailors interpreting wave patterns, the behaviors of birds and fish, the movements of winds and clouds, the sun during the day, and the constellations at night—that enabled Pacific islanders to find their islands in the first place, then voyage among them with confidence. It is thought that Polynesian navigation systems date back at least three thousand years.

In China the familiar square sail was developed with many battens of wood or bamboo across it—the standard sail of Chinese junks today and for nearly a thousand years prior. This was a manageable

A big lateen sail brings plenty of power to this fishing boat on the coast of Kenya.

A typical Chinese junk's battened sails move a boxy hull. Despite their paper-lantern look, these sails are tough and efficient.

sail that always held its shape, could function as a square sail with the wind behind or as an airfoil with the wind to the side or to some degree in front, and could be shortened almost instantly by dropping it down by degrees. In heavier wind or a storm, a junk sail can be collapsed like a reverse venetian blind.

The great boxy ships of the Chinese were trading with the Philippines and the coasts and islands of Southeast Asia more than a thousand years ago, running west before the wind outbound, then sailing back to China when the wind direction reversed itself. At the same time, the bravest of Arab traders sailed east in their lateen-rigged vessels to do business in Southeast Asia and China.

EARLY EUROPEAN VOYAGERS

Sailors a thousand years ago were becoming familiar with seasonal and regional wind patterns, enough so that trade routes were growing longer. Traders and sailors were more confident in the winds that would fill their sails and in the capabilities of all their voyaging technology—sails, spars, rigging, vessels, and indeed their own skills.

The most daring sailors of the years A.D. 800 to 1100 were the Vikings, whose elegant, canoelike longships carried a big square sail that could be cocked into the wind to draw the vessel forward. Beginning as pirates with raids down to England and France in the late 700s and early 800s, the Vikings even-

A fat Mediterranean carrack surfs before blasts of wind that tear her sails in this early-fifteenth-century painting of St. Nicholas calming a storm.

tually sailed their longships to Ireland, the Mediterranean, Iceland, and North America. Swedish Vikings rowed and sailed down the rivers of what is now Russia and pursued trade and conquest in the Black Sea and in a place they called Grikkland (Greece). And former Danish Vikings—now speaking French and living in Normandy (the land of the North Men)—conquered England in 1066. They arrived in a fleet of sailing longships. The Vikings were not the sophisticated navigators that the South Sea islanders were (among other gambits, the Vikings let loose caged ravens when they needed to find land, and watched where the birds flew), but they were great ship and sail handlers. It is remarkable that they made the voyages they did in wild northern seas and weather in ships that were lightly built and had only one sail. Many Viking ships must have been lost at sea.

When things settled down in northern Europe, the traders and politicians of ports in Germany, Holland, Belgium, England, and Scandinavia formed leagues to regulate trade, fight pirates, and develop better ships and port facilities. The most famous of these was the

OPPOSITE: A replica of John Cabot's *Matthew* sails in a 1990s gathering of historic ships. Vessels like *Matthew*, well-manned and with multiple sails, made the Age of Discovery possible. ABOVE: Norman ships sail to England in 1066 under fanciful squaresails in this detail from the Bayeux Tapestry. These were Viking ships, and the Normans were former Danish Vikings.

Hanseatic League, organized in North Germany in the 1200s and an influence on ships and shipping for four hundred years. Ships in medieval Europe grew larger and more capable, with heavy construction, rounder and huskier hulls, and several sails. These were the ancestors of the ships and sail arrangements that came along quickly after Columbus. The Hanseatic hulk of the 1400s had three masts with square sails on the two forward and a lateen sail on the mizzen. This was much like the sail arrangement of Portugal's caravels.

Multisail rigs were the future for large vessels—they made it possible to raise a spread of sail in light weather, shorten down in heavy wind, use one or several small sails to maneuver in port, or ride through a storm with a scrap of sail forward to keep the vessel's motion and steering predictable.

The variety of sails and sailing arrangements that have come along during the past five hundred years, especially in Europe, is astonishing. These have been five hundred years of what we like to call progress, with European ships sailing every sea; with fishermen harvesting the deep for everything from shrimp to tuna; with a variety of local sailing types doing their work and making their reputations all over the world; with populations growing and demanding products and food from afar—including dried and salted codfish caught by English, Dutch, French, Basque, Spanish, and Portuguese fishermen off the coasts of North America; and with the world shrinking and nations coming into contact as never before.

A galleon in all her gilded glory is the focus of this seventeenth-century painting by Jan Beecq. Having discovered, then conquered, the world, European trading nations defended their territories and imported foreign luxuries in great ships like these.

Sails and sailing vessels made possible the abundant and interconnected world we know today. From a leafy branch raised by the skipper of a dugout canoe in hopes of a breeze to the two dozen sails on a clipper ship of 1850 booming along at twenty knots (38kph) before a trade wind, sails and sailing have transformed the world.

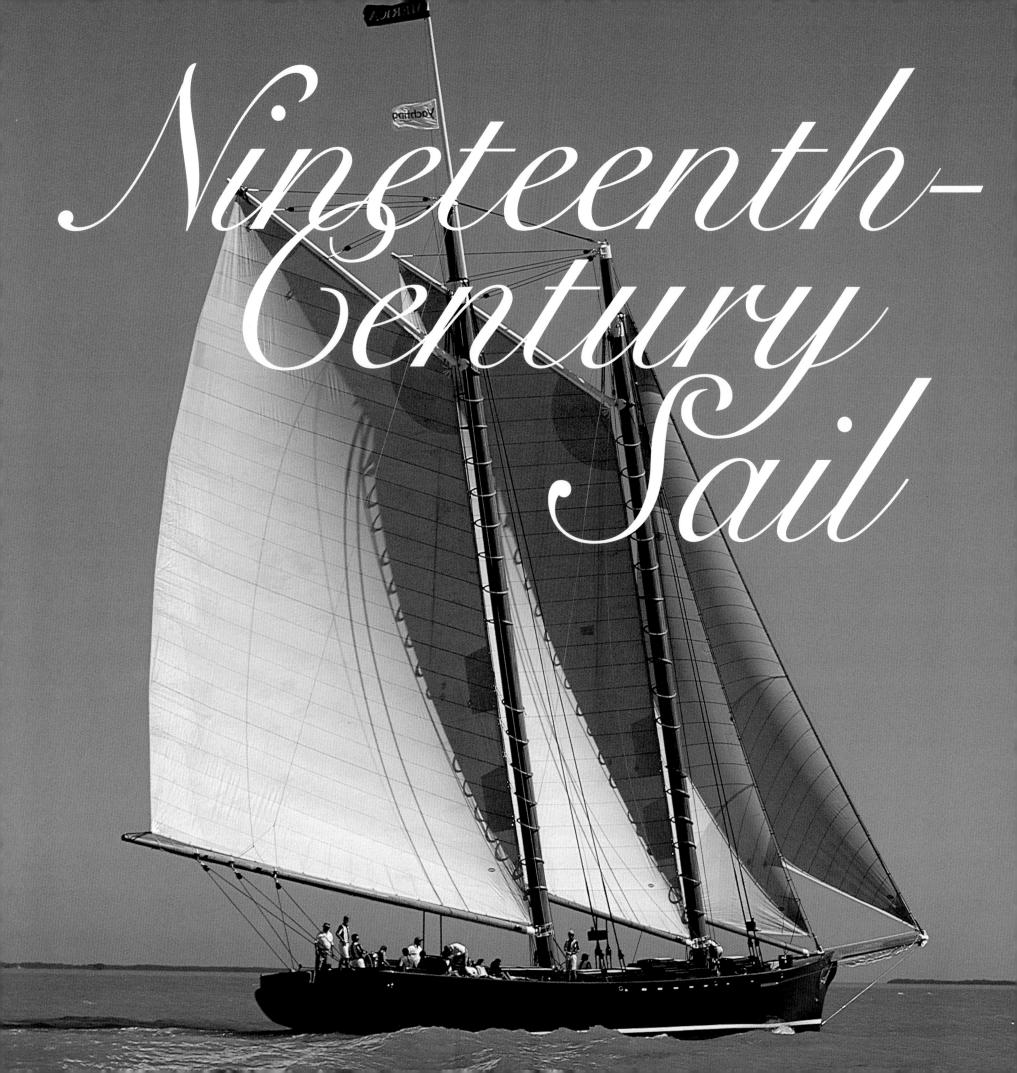

Nineteenth-Century Sail

SAILS AND SAILING REACHED SEVERAL ULTIMATES DURING THE NINETEENTH CENTURY. CERTAINLY IN TERMS OF NUMBERS THIS WAS THE GREAT CENTURY OF SAIL, AND IN TERMS OF BEAUTY AND EFFICIENCY THE WORLD'S SAILING VESSELS ACHIEVED A PERFECTION STILL ADMIRED TODAY.

Also ultimate was the sense of being the end. Although a diminishing fleet of sailing vessels carried cargo and caught fish in much of the world halfway into the twentieth century, and the smaller and nimbler vessels of the nineteenth century were models for many of the yachts of the twentieth, sail was a dying technology by the late 1800s.

Steam vessels, independent of the wind and increasingly reliable as the century moved on, took ever more of the world's cargo and passenger business on bays and rivers as well as out in the ocean. By 1880 steamships were carrying more of the world's sea cargo than sailing ships, and by 1880 two German engineers had devised a little engine that produced power when an explosion pushed a piston inside a cylinder. Steam took the wind out of the sails of deep-water ships, and the explosive machine we now know as the gasoline engine replaced sail in a variety of small vessels all over the world.

Sailing ships and local boats continue to carry cargo and catch fish in older and more conservative places on Earth—India, Egypt, Brazil, Indonesia, the South Pacific—but engine power is still replacing sail power. Aboard the big lumber schooners of Indonesia's Java Sea, the sailors dream of engines, talk of engines, and await the day when a diesel will deliver them from the hard work of sailing a hundred-foot (30m) ship with creaky rigging and patched sails.

A replica of the 1851 schooner yacht *America* shows the crisp set of her sails on a Florida cruise. Rakish schooners like her were favored by nineteenth-century yachtsmen in America and in Europe.

Chapter Two

Nevertheless, most of the world misses its tall ships and coasting schooners, fishing smacks and sailing canoes. They were vehicles of romance in every way, and nostalgia for them is the reason for the success of events like Operation Sail, for new maritime museums being established nearly everywhere, and for the strong market in yachts and small boats that are replicas or derivations of traditional sailing types.

Nineteenth-century types are the most favored. They are sleeker, more manageable, and perhaps most of all more familiar than older and clumsier vessels. Who would have a colonial New England schooner for a cruising yacht when they could have a variation on the 1851 schooner yacht *America* or a yacht inspired by one of Tom McManus' 1890s fishing vessels? The romance we have with classic sailboats in the twentieth century is inspired by paintings, Currier & Ives lithographs, and port and resort photographs, as well as actual ships and small boats of the nineteenth century that have fortunately been preserved in maritime museums all over the world. (Only a few examples of ships and boats from before 1800 have survived.)

OPPOSITE: A classic Fife cutter from the turn of the century spreads a cloud of gaff-rigged sail. ABOVE: New York sand-baggers race at Robbins Reef in this watercolor by Fred Cozzens. In the background is a small cutter yacht, at right a lug-rigged sailing canoe. All three were typical small Long Island Sound sailboats in the 1880s.

VESSEL TYPES

At the beginning of the nineteenth century more ships and more boats were built because of expanding populations, especially in the Americas; because of an end to the wars at sea that had engaged European nations and snarled sea commerce since the discovery of America; and because of the Industrial Revolution, which made it easier to produce goods and exploit natural resources. Two hundred years ago, more and better sailing machines were not only possible due to new tools and other resources, they were necessary. If the nineteenth century was a hundred years of sails and sailing advancement—from the two-man fishing boats that inspired the small recreational sailboats we know today to the clippers with their clouds of sail that discovered and exploited the trade routes and trade winds that today's ocean-cruising sailors follow—it was because there was plenty of work for sailing vessels to do. The sheer volume of coal to be hauled around the world (much of it, ironically, to be burned by steamers); lumber from Africa, Asia, and the Americas to be transported to places where suitable trees were in short supply; grain by the shipload to be brought to starving millions; manufactured goods to be exchanged for grain or lumber and brought by ship; shrimp to be netted; mackerel to be hooked; oysters to be dredged—all this kept sailors busy, skillful, and inventive.

The vessels that did the work were smart developments of types that had evolved before 1800. When multiple sails came into favor in China, the Arab world, and Europe in place of bigger single sails that were less versatile and often hard to manage, the evolution of a variety of sailing rigs escalated, especially in Europe. Ketches—vessels

Typical nineteenth-century vessels are shown in a British painting of the period, including several cutter yachts, a topsail schooner, and a brigantine.

that have two masts with the smaller mast aft and the largest sail on the mainmast—are thought to have appeared in Scandinavia during the Middle Ages. Local types from Egypt, Arabia, and India have a similar rig with two lateen sails. Schooners—vessels that have two or more masts of equal height with fore-and-aft sails of equal size, or two masts with the largest sail on the aftermast—are credited to Dutch sailors of the 1600s. A sloop is a single-masted vessel with a triangular jib set

forward of the mast and a big fore-and-aft mainsail set aft of the mast. This rig is credited to the Dutch (the word "sloop" itself is Dutch) although, as with the schooner, there are Scandinavian claims as well. The cutter, a type popular in Britain, is a sloop variation with two or more foresails and a mast near the center of the hull. The catboat is an American invention of the nineteenth century, although the simple little boats with spritsails that seem to date back to the Romans are obvious ancestors.

Larger vessels with more and larger sails came along as developments of the cogs and hulks of northern Europe's Middle Ages, the caravels of the Mediterranean, the Arab dhows, and the Chinese junks. In the nineteenth century some of them became legends for their beauty, efficiency, or speed: the Baltimore schooners, the fast packets and clippers of mid-century, the British tea clippers, the French West India vessels, the Baltic traders, and the coasting vessels of many nations.

RECREATIONAL BOATS

The charm of nineteenth-century sail was not limited to commercial vessels. Smaller vessels of the nineteenth century became legends, too, especially among yachtsmen. Many of these vessels were yachtlike already, fancier and more luxurious than other working boats. Most were just the right size—less than one hundred feet (30m)—for the adventures of a recreational sailor and his family. And all had the romance of nineteenth-century working sail in their details—bowsprits, carved nameboards, gaff sails, and interesting rigging to play with. Catboats, cat ketches, pinky schooners, sloop boats, and sailing yawlboats were among the working types that the

yachtsmen of the twentieth century either bought used from fishermen who were building new boats (after 1900, many of these were new boats with engines) or adopted as models for new construction.

For much of the twentieth century these workboat-style yachts were called "character boats," sometimes because they had character, often because they were owned by characters. In the 1950s and 1960s, owners of boats that looked like something in a Winslow Homer painting received snickers from their more contemporary contemporaries. In the 1980s and 1990s, the revival of interest in traditional boats caused such boats of character and historical interest—and their owners as well—to be admired rather than dismissed. They were admired at classic and antique boat shows, in the pages of the boating magazines, and in marinas where ninety-nine percent of the other boats were plastic products of the past forty years, boats that served their purposes well enough but hardly ever turned heads. Traditional sailboats turn heads and start conversations. They are not everybody's cup of rum-sweetened tea (especially older wooden boats, whose upkeep requires skill and diligence), but they may be nearly everybody's favorite sailboats for their aesthetic qualities, their historic connections, and indeed for the romance they embody and inspire.

Some of the nineteenth century's small boats were working boats deliberately rebuilt or rerigged as yachts, as boats for weekend fun. In America, yachting and sailboat racing were pursued from the beginning by people at both the upper and lower ends of the waterfront's social scale. By the middle of the century, the yacht club members raced big sloops and schooners, while at the same time workmen and fishermen in ports like Philadelphia and New York raced small sloops and bird-shooting boats. Blue-collar racing and yachting were so much fun that eventually the blue-blazer crowd wanted to play the game. Oliver Iselin, the New York Yacht Club's Rear Commodore in 1890 and a major figure in America's Cup campaigns between 1893 and 1903, also owned and raced sandbaggers on New York Harbor in the 1870s and 1880s.

A replica sharpie with cat-ketch rig—two big triangular sails on a broad shallow hull—sails at Mystic Seaport, where it was built. Boats like this served bay fisheries from Rhode Island to the Carolinas in the last half of the nineteenth century.

The sandbaggers were extreme versions of the clamming and oystering sloops that fished the bays around New York, much as Formula One race cars are extreme versions of sports cars. What began as informal races among watermen in their working sloops and catboats soon escalated into weekend contests among built-for-racing boats crewed by waterfront musclemen, boats frequently owned or sponsored by saloons. The sandbaggers, named for the fifty- to seventy-five-pound (23 to 34kg) bags of sand that were shifted from one side of the boat to the other when the little racer changed tacks, were ultimately very broad and very shallow boats with so much sail that long bowsprits forward and boomkins aft extended out to about as much extra length as the hull itself. The rig extended even farther. Hence the need for the sandbags—only the weight of the sandbags and the Bowery Boys who wrestled them from one rail to the other kept the boat from capsizing.

When these boats raced in New York Harbor and Long Island Sound in the 1870s and 1880s, their courses were followed by excursion boats filled with thousands of paying customers, who, along with the owners, placed large cash bets on the result of each race. A report of an 1870 sandbagger race

had this to say: "The odds before the start were 100 to 80 on *Bella*, and it was estimated that over $50,000 was placed in outside bets. The steamboat *Sylvan Grove* carried a large party from New York, and took aboard much of the population of Bridgeport; the town was en fête, with the Bridgeport band, flags flown everywhere ashore, and not only yachts but working vessels displaying all the bunting they could muster." Sailboat racing has not been anywhere near as popular since.

Similar boats were raced on the Delaware River at Philadelphia before 1860, but the principal racing there involved smaller boats—racing versions of Delaware River and Delaware Bay duck-hunting sloops and catboats. These were Delaware Duckers, about fifteen feet (4.5m) long, each with three crew balancing a small hull and a big single sail, and boats called "hikers" and "tuckups" that took the concept further with larger sails and with crews of three or four using their weight to oppose the force of the wind. To get more of their weight out farther to windward, they hung out on trapeze lines from the masthead with their feet planted on the rail. Alternatively, crews balanced on planks rigged out to windward, a method of capsize control common on Chesapeake Bay's racing log canoes, another extreme type from the 1880s.

OPPOSITE: **The replica Block Island cowhorn** *Glory Anna* **sails at Mystic Seaport. Deep, husky cat-ketches like this one harvested fish in the ocean.** ABOVE: **The New York Yacht Club regatta of 1868 brings nearly a dozen boats to the starting line in this Currier & Ives lithograph. Before television, movies, and vaudeville, such events were a public entertainment.**

WORKING BOATS

On the working waterfront, the nineteenth century's list of graceful, fast, commodious, and otherwise attractive small sailing boats is long and sometimes legendary: sloop boats like the lobstering vessels of Maine or the Connecticut smacks that fished from Long Island Sound to the Florida Keys, all of them with the style of miniature clipper ships; catboats in various sizes to about thirty feet (9m), built for shellfishing and adopted by yachtsmen; wherries and Whitehall boats for harbor errands and recreational excursions; dories with spritsails for harvesting the fishing banks of the Atlantic or, in one gentrification, rigged with jib and mainsail for Boston and Salem gentlemen to race; English lapstrake dinghies from the working waterfront that became the inspiration for many of the world's small racing sailboats; flat-board boats like the sharpies and sharpie skiffs of the Long Island Sound oyster fishery; husky double-enders like the Tancook Whalers and the Block Island Cowhorns; or the vee-bottom skipjacks of the Cheseapeake with their clipper details and big sailplans on raked masts.

All of these classic sailing workboats have been replicated or reinterpreted, sometimes in fiberglass, or in some rare instances restored and rebuilt as yachts for recreational sailors of romantic inclination—characters who choose to own character boats. One of the most romantic examples of this is *Black Pearl*, a seventy-foot (21m) hermaphrodite brig, yacht-size but similar in miniature to the

Two nineteenth-century types that began as working vessels and soon attracted recreational sailors are the Chesapeake Bay log canoe and the Cape Cod catboat. The log canoe above, with sails down, is an original that races on weekends. The catboat *Breck Marshall*, at left, is a replica that takes Mystic Seaport visitors for summer sails.

brigs that adventured and traded around the world in the first half of the nineteenth century. Social and historical organizations for owners and admirers of some of these boats exist in the United States, such as the Catboat Association, the Friendship Sloop Society, the Chesapeake Bay Sailing Log Canoe Association, the Sharpie Association, and the Traditional Small Craft Association.

HISTORICAL REPLICAS

Some nineteenth-century classics have been replicated by historical, environmental, educational, and even government organizations. The Hudson River sloop *Clearwater*, an interpretation of the big sloops that carried passengers and cargo on the river all during the nineteenth century, was built in 1969 for an environmental foundation whose mission was to clean up the Hudson. *Clearwater* has been sailing the river ever since as a vehicle for environmental and historical education. Her big sails are seen on the river from Albany down to Staten Island, and they turn the heads of romantics and cynics alike. *Clearwater* is, like all the replica vessels that have come along during the past forty years, something dramatic and real to remind us of what once was—bays and harbors and rivers full of sails.

The Baltimore schooners of the nineteenth century were fast, agile little ships that were acquired and imitated all over the world as dispatch and antismuggling vessels in the navies of Sweden, France, Britain, and the United States; as vehicles for smugglers and slavers who did not intend to get caught; as pirate vessels in the first few decades of the nineteenth century; and as fast cargo carriers for goods like flour and fruit that might spoil aboard slower ships. The replica Baltimore schooners *Pride of Baltimore I* and *Pride of Baltimore II* were built by the city of Baltimore as goodwill vessels to advertise this important U.S. port.

Another Chesapeake type—a beamier development of the so-called Baltimore clippers—is what was called a Pungy schooner on the waterfronts of Chesapeake Bay. These graceful schooners carried cargo up and down the bay during the nineteenth century, and sometimes went farther—down to the Bahamas to load pineapples, all the way to Jamaica for coffee or bananas. *Lady Maryland* is a

RIGHT: **The replica Hudson River sloop** *Clearwater* **spreads her big gaff mainsail on her home river with the towering Manhattan skyline in the background.** OPPOSITE: **The second** *Pride of Baltimore,* **a replica Baltimore schooner, spreads mainsail, foresail, two headsails, and a square topsail, just like her predecessors of the 1830s.**

lovely replica of one of these schooners, owned by the State of Maryland and based in Baltimore, where she keeps a busy schedule taking Maryland schoolchildren out on the bay for environmental and marine biological trips.

Spirit of Massachusetts, built in 1984 on the model of the clipper-style fishing schooners that sailed to the Grand Banks in the 1880s, is another vessel for environmental education and another good example of nineteenth-century working sail. She is owned by the New England Historic Seaport of Boston and makes sail-training, sea science, and similar voyages for her owners and for other organizations. She is one of the most beautiful of the replica vessels that have been launched all over the world since the 1960s.

Harvey Gamage, named for the celebrated Maine shipwright who built her in 1973, is an approximation of the coasting schooners that carried goods on all U.S. coasts, including the Great Lakes, during the nineteenth century. There were tens of thousands of these schooners—the eighteen-wheel trucks of their time—carrying building materials and lumber down from Maine and maritime Canada, fruit up the coast from the West Indies, coal from Newport News to Boston, or furniture from cities in Michigan to cities on the East Coast. Another coasting-schooner type is *Bill of Rights*, built by Harvey Gamage in 1971. She is now part of the fleet of VisionQuest, a training program for young people who have had crime, drug, or other problems and who benefit from the discipline and confidence learned in sailing this 134-foot (41m) traditional and beautiful ship.

One of the most spectacular re-creations of a nineteenth-century sailing vessel is *Californian*, launched in 1984 as an interpretation of the U.S. revenue cutters that were built in the first half of the nineteenth century to chase smugglers on all coasts of the United States. A big topsail schooner of 125 tons (113t) that is reminiscent of the Gold Rush revenue vessel *Joe Lane*, *Californian* is owned and operated by the Nautical Heritage Museum of Dana Point, California. She is California's official tall ship, and makes educational cruises with crews of young cadets, as many of the world's sail-training vessels do.

All of these replicas, re-creations, and reinterpretations of nineteenth-century yachts and working vessels bring back something admirable and beautiful from a lost world that modern people seem to dream about. Indeed, as the century turns yet again, many people look wistfully at what seem to have been simpler yet more elegant times. But the world in which our forebears lived a hundred and more years ago included sixty-hour work weeks, a minimal amount of what we would consider proper hygiene, a diet that depended on seasonal agriculture, horse manure in the streets, unreliable heat in houses, and limited goods in stores. But it also included sailing ships and lively little gaff-rigged yachts on the waterways and in the harbors, scenes of sails large and small that produce a powerful sense of nostalgia.

We miss those sail-filled vistas and busy harbors. Sailing vessels bringing drama to the horizon or going through their everyday harbor maneuvers—a dance of sail as they luff up to a waiting tug, sheer off on a good breeze to avoid colliding with a ferry, or drop all sail with way on to drift into a dock—are gone from our ports and river landings, replaced now by less graceful things like railroad cars and tractor-trailers.

Opposite: *Bill of Rights*, a replica schooner built in 1971, is reminiscent of the small sailing cargo vessels that were the eighteen-wheel trucks of nineteenth-century America's coastal trade. Above: Deck gear and furniture aboard *Spirit of Massachusetts* is authentic right down to the ship's wheel, made by the same foundry that produced hardware for schooners a century ago.

The vessels of the nineteenth century are mostly gone. But they are not forgotten, as the replicas and reinterpretations in these pages make clear. Even the newer boats in succeeding chapters owe their debt, and often their style, to nineteenth-century types. There is something about them: undeniable gracefulness, the kick of letting the wind do the work, the recognition that all the wonderful things they do are done with human wit and muscle. There is also the tactile and visual appreciation of what the traditional types are made of—hemp and canvas and wood and paint and varnish—all somehow more sympathetic to humans than metal and plastic. A lot of basic things attract us to sailing vehicles, especially to the old types and rigs, from English dinghies to coasting schooners. It isn't easy to explain. But it doesn't need to be explained.

OPPOSITE and RIGHT: Simple in stucture and complex in design and use, the rigging of sailing vessels withstands the power of the wind and works with it in sophisticated ways.

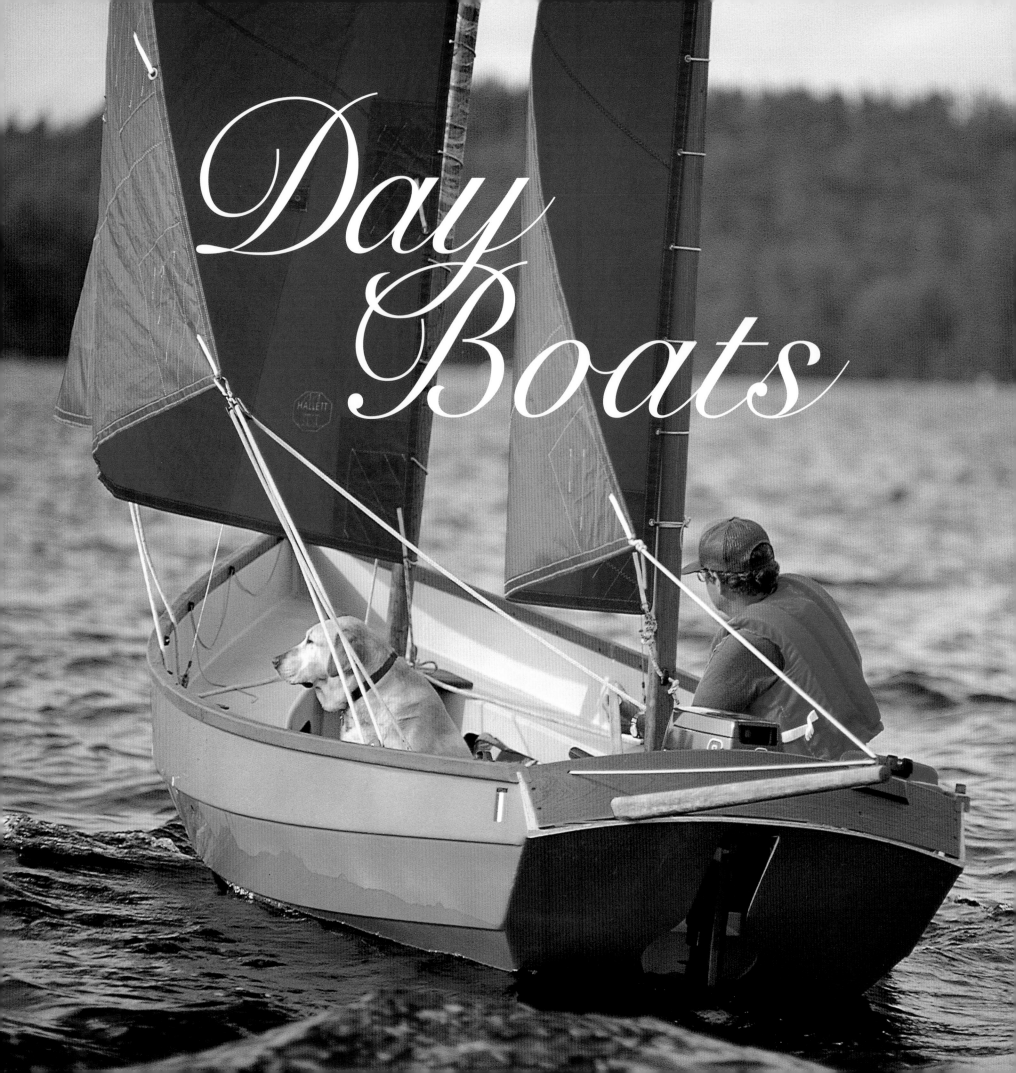

Day
Boats

DAY BOATS ARE EXACTLY THAT—BOATS TO BE ENJOYED BETWEEN SUNUP AND SUNDOWN, BOATS WHOSE FOCUS IS ONE SIMPLE EXPERIENCE: SAILING DOWN THE HARBOR ON A FAINT MORNING BREEZE TO SEE WHAT BIGGER YACHTS HAVE COME IN TO ANCHOR SINCE YESTERDAY, SHOWING UP FOR AN AFTERNOON RACE AND THE CAMARADERIE THAT

accompanies it, or stirring for an hour or two from the porch of a summer cottage on a breezy afternoon to sail a big exhilarating circle around the lake. In larger cruising boats the focus may be the boat itself—how the sails are setting, whether the auxiliary engine needs a new battery, or how much ice is left on top of the beer and cold cuts. Or the concentration may be on the progress of the cruise—where a good anchorage might be an hour or two later, what tomorrow's weather will bring, whether to head back or keep going.

Sailing a day boat centers on the day or the hour's promise and the day's water and weather. The promise may be wind enough to go all the way across the bay and back without getting becalmed; the weather may be brisk enough to try yourself and the boat while risking some trouble. Either way it's you, a little boat, and the sailing skills you keep right on learning. Like the boat itself, the experience is simpler and closer to certain realities than cruising. The water is closer to the senses—close enough to reach out and touch; the sail is closer to the hand—a few feet of rope away; the day is closer in the mind. When they're good ones, you remember such days with surprising clarity.

People have been having good day-boat experiences for ages. Before the nineteenth century, most such people were waterfront workmen on various errands or fishermen sailing to nearby fishing grounds or tending traps. Some of the pleasure and adventure of the work must have been the sailing part. Doing it for recreation is a recent phenomenon, although it is

A sailor and his dog go for a daysail on Sebago Lake, Maine, in a ketch-rigged open boat with the look of England's North Sea coast.

not hard to imagine Egyptian or Roman fishermen filling their boats with family for an afternoon of playful sailing. Something like this was almost certainly a feature of waterfront life through the ages on coasts and lakes and rivers. Then the nineteenth century's combinations of a little extra money and leisiure time for tradesmen, a lot of extra money and leisure time for some of the tycoons, and an explosion of good boatbuilding technology and materials—at least in America—made such recreational sailing a common phenomenon.

DORIES, CATBOATS, AND SKIFFS

Some of the boats and boat types that were sailed for pleasure a century ago are still sailed for pleasure today. Dories and dory skiffs are simple, frequently home-built boats that today's recreational sailors may favor for their associations with North Atlantic fishing, for their lively sailing behavior, or for their plain good looks. The Marblehead dory skiff shown in these pages, built in Mystic Seaport's boat shop, is an especially able and elegant little dory type, able to be sailed, rowed, or pushed by a small outboard. Although this boat is only thirteen feet five inches (4m) long and four feet one inch (1.2m) wide, that guru of the traditional boat

movement throughout the world, John Gardner, has said of it, "For a rowing sea boat, you can't do much better within the fourteen-foot [4.2m] limit." Plans for the Marblehead dory skiff are available from Mystic Seaport's Waterfront Plans Collection at the museum in Mystic, Connecticut.

Another elegant, and in fact gentrified, dory is the larger Beachcomber-Alpha, a twenty-one-foot (6.4m) variation of Massachusetts North Shore fishing dories created by renowned Marblehead boatbuilder William Chamberlain for the Beachcomber Club of Marblehead and the Alpha Dory Club of Salem. These were boats for not fishermen but gentlemen to race, which they did early in the twentieth century. The Beachcomber-Alpha is still around, still a successful day boat in backyard-built versions created from plans in John Gardner's *The Dory Book* or from plans and kits sold by Glen-L Marine of California.

The dory and its derivative, the dory skiff, are a day-boat type that dates back to the nineteenth century. This fourteen-foot (4.3m) Marblehead dory skiff was built at Mystic Seaport.

Catboats—favored nineteenth-century recreational types—are still to be found on traditional-boat waterfronts, especially in New England. The classic cat-rigged day boat—if the definition of classic excludes Lasers, Sunfish, and all other single-mainsail boats of the plastic era—is the Beetle Cat, a twelve-foot-four-inch (3.7m) boat designed and first built in the middle of the 1920s but based on much earlier examples. Beetle Cats are still built in wood by the Concordia Company of South Dartmouth, Massachusetts, and they seem to be nothing less than cult objects. Jacqueline Onassis kept one to sail in the Greek islands; celebrity sailors enjoy them on Georgica Pond in the currently chic Hamptons on Long Island, New York; and ordinary cottagers and lazy-afternoon sailors find them just the vehicles for any-time-of-daysailing—no racing, no fuss, and only one sail to handle.

There are other boats like this—day boats that are true to the promise of the type, which is more or less "Get in the boat, get the sail up, and get going." Most other sailing machines are more complicated. Sailing skiffs are uncomplicated in every way; they are the plain wooden rowboats of the nineteenth and twentieth centuries made into simple sailing machines with the addition of a centerboard—to keep them steered straight and not sideways—and a manageable and portable sailing rig with either a single sail or jib-and-mainsail on a single mast. Like the simplest dories, the simplest of these flatiron skiffs—named for the domestic device they resemble—are built from wide boards and a few sawed frames. And like many dories, some of these skiffs are sur-

OPPOSITE: Another classic day boat with nineteenth-century roots is the small open catboat. A successful survivor of the type is the Beetle Cat, a graceful little boat still being built in the 1990s. RIGHT: This daysailing catboat shows off her shine and her finely-fitted wood.

prisingly handsome. A few years ago *WoodenBoat* magazine conducted a design contest for simple skiffs. All of the finalists were good-looking variations on the flatiron theme, and the winner is a boat that anyone with wood-butchery skills, patience, and a few hundred dollars should be able to build. As a day boat for learning sailing skills, knocking around a local waterway when the powerboats aren't out, sailing off for a picnic, or many more days or hours of adventuring, a little boat like this is ideal. Drawings and specifications for what *WoodenBoat* calls the Perfect Skiff are available from the WoodenBoat Store in Brooklin, Maine.

DINGHIES AND OTHER CLASSIC DAYSAILERS

Some other day boats are more complicated in their construction, rigging, or behavior. All the little racing flatirons and dinghies—Blue Jays, Comets, Snipes, Lightnings, Dyer sailing dinghies, and International 14s—may be enjoyed as day boats even though their purpose is racing. The older, wooden versions of these one-design classes tend to go to pasture, like horses, and take up a recreational life when they no longer compete.

This is a boon to the no-schedule sailor willing to maintain a wooden boat that may be made of Honduras mahogany or other furniture-grade woods. It is a boon so long as the sailor knows what he or she may be getting for a very low price—a great day boat from the past that was built by craftsmen; a boat whose wood requires dry storage every winter; a boat that should get renewed paint and varnish and linseed oil every spring, careful attention to keeping the bilges dry all summer, and a good cleanup of mildew and moisture pockets in the fall when the boat gets stored. Fiberglass boats get hosed off and turned over in the fall, and that's the end of it until they get hosed off and turned over again in the spring. Wooden boats—even very small ones—need more of an owner's attention. Maintaining a small wooden boat can be relaxing and creative, but owners of varnished and painted wooden dinghies will be thankful that they are not owners of varnished and painted wooden cruising boats. At the same time, and against all logic, they will dream of being owners of varnished and painted wooden cruising boats.

Brand-new day boats of fiberglass have few maintenance requirements even if they show off quantities of wood trim, although every year—and more frequently in the tropics—the oiled or varnished wood needs to be touched up. Brand-new day boats of wood are often as maintenance-free as plastic boats today thanks to—oddly enough—a plastic. Epoxy resin is widely used in boatbuilding now as a glue, as a chemical that impregnates and hardens wood in the same way that a fiberglass boat's polyester resin impregnates and hardens layers of glass cloth, and as a gloss finish. The fully epoxied wooden boat will have the finish of furniture and the durability of a pickup truck.

A few good examples of this are Edey and Duff's Sakonnet 23, the Bridges Point 24 from the Bridges Point Boatyard in Maine, and Cape Cod Shipbuilding's twenty-one-foot (6.4m) Marlin, a fiberglass version of Nathanael Herreshoff's graceful Fish Class sloop, first built in wood in 1916. All three of these boats have fiberglass hulls, but their early-twentieth-century shapes and considerable varnished-wood trim nicely conceal their plastic essences. They are sailing classics, whatever they're made from—the Sakonnet a canoe-form double-ender designed by Joel White for fast and responsive

A Lightning one-design is enjoyed on a daysail past Portland Lighthouse on Casco Bay, Maine.

sailing, the Marlin an admirable re-creation of Captain Nat's husky full-keel daysailer, a boat allegedly based on nineteenth-century West Indian fishing sloops. The Bridges Point 24, another Joel White design, is built as an open-cockpit daysailer or as an overnighter with a cuddy cabin that shelters a vee berth and a head. As an interpretation of the many classic day boats sponsored by yacht clubs, she brings back a type from the last decades of the nineteenth century and the first decades of the twentieth.

Beginning in the 1880s, when middle-class yacht clubs were flourishing all over the country and racing small sailboats was one of the enjoyments, many clubs commissioned the design and construction of their own racing and daysailing boat—usually a jib-and-mainsail boat from twenty to thirty feet (6 to 9.1m), and usually with a small rounded-front cabin trunk that nicely complemented the bladelike shape of the bow and the gentle curve of the sheerline. The cabin might contain two

Edey and Duff's canoe-form Sakonnet 23, designed by Joel White, is a lively fiberglass day boat with the look of wood and canvas.

berths, but it was really for sail stowage and occasional refuge from wind and rain. Building a fleet of all the same boats served two purposes: it reduced the per-boat cost by giving a local boatbuilder a rare series-production opportunity as club members committed for boats, and it made the subsequent racing as fair as possible because all the boats had the same hulls, gear, and sails. These were early one-design classes. They were also elegant boats, and because not many originals are still around—with the exception of a few New England yacht clubs still racing their old fleets—the type is now being widely replicated and reinterpreted.

Dinghies and yacht tenders are classic day boats for rowing around shallow backwaters or hoisting sail in a moderate breeze for a trip to town from the anchored big boat or for an impromptu sail to noplace in particular. "Dinghy" is a Hindi word for "small boat" that the British navy adopted and brought back to England. The earliest dinghies were British—fat little boats less than fifteen feet (4.5m) with rounded lines, flat sheerlines, great capacities for their sizes, and uncomplicated rigs with spritsails, lugsails, single mainsails, or mainsails accompanied by a small jib. Good examples of the type being built today or able to be built in the family garage are the Dyer sailing dinghies made from fiberglass in the United States, Iain Oughtred's inspired designs for several sizes of

Bathtubby but beloved, the fiberglass Dyer dinghies have been favorite day boats for yachtsmen and young yacht-club sailors like this one since the 1950s.

Acorn dinghies, and Joel White's Shellback and Catspaw dinghies, both of which can be built from plans sold by the WoodenBoat Store in Maine.

The Dyers, based on English-dinghy models and originally built in wood, are classics even in their postwar fiberglass evolution. Given varnished wood trim and handsome bronze hardware, they hardly look like plastic boats. Dyer sailing dinghies are built in seven-foot-eleven-inch, nine-foot, ten-foot, and twelve-foot-six-inch (2.4, 2.7, 3, and 3.8m) lengths. They are much favored as tenders for bigger cruising yachts and as dinghy-racing vehicles for yacht clubs in North America. Iain Oughtred's Acorns, in sizes from seven feet ten inches to fifteen feet (2.3 to 4.5m), are meant to be home-built from strakes of eight-millimeter marine plywood sprung around a few laminated frames and finished off with a mahogany transom. The glued laps afford these boats wonderful strength for their weights—only a hundred pounds (45.5kg) for the eleven-foot-nine-inch (3.5m) boat—and also give them the pleasing aesthetics of rounded-form lapstrake hulls. The designer sells plans for these boats from his base in Scotland, and Acorn plans are available in North America from the WoodenBoat Store.

OPPOSITE: Children sail their Snipe one-design on Long Island Sound, enjoying a post-race excursion on a breezy afternoon. BELOW: The Shellback dinghy is a daysailer designed by Joel White for home construction.

Joel White's designs for several small wooden dinghies are that rare thing—a rethinking of something classic that may even be an improvement. His eleven-foot-two-inch (3.4m) Shellback dinghy is a simplified dory skiff with saucy curves and a small lugsail. His twelve-foot-eight-inch (3.8m) Catspaw dinghy is a traditional carvel-planked hull with a spritsail. Both are available in plan form from the WoodenBoat Store, which also has a kit for the Shellback.

Canoe yawls are classic day boats that originated in the 1880s in England as elegant canoe-form hulls with yawl rigs—jib-and-mainsail accompanied by a small jigger all the way aft—and were

Opposite: *Grimalkin* is another minicruiser and daysailer based on a nineteenth-century design—in this case, Commodore Ralph Munro's twenty-eight-foot (8.5m) shallow-draft cat-ketch. Above: William Garden's canoe yawl *Eel* is a shapely mini-cruiser and daysailer inspired by English types from a hundred years ago.

enjoyed by ladies and gentlemen on daylight excursions and sometimes overnight camp-outs. English canoe yawls flourished between the 1880s and the 1920s, and their owners used them for adventurous day trips and cruises along the North Sea and English Channel coasts. William Garden's Eel design is an eighteen-foot-six-inch (5.6m) update on the old theme, a boat for the enjoyment of manipulating the three small sails and appreciating the subtle aesthetics of the hull with its canoe ends and appendages—bowsprit forward and little boomkin aft. Another canoe-and-two-sail combination (this one not a canoe yawl) is Bob Baker's Piccolo design, a twelve-foot-eight-inch (3.8m) sailing canoe with two small and simple standing lugsails in ketch configuration. Piccolo is meant to be home-built with quarter-inch (6mm) lapstrake planking in a choice of woods on fine frames of oak or ash. This is not a simple boatbuilding project, but the delicate hull that results is breathtaking. Plans for Baker's Piccolo and Garden's Eel are available from the WoodenBoat Store in Maine.

Two outstanding examples of larger day boats are *Grimalkin*, a yacht version of the New Haven sharpies noted in the previous chapter, and *Patrician*, a very large day boat with berths

A lavishly sized day boat, the beautiful *Patrician*. ABOVE and OPPOSITE, designed by Henry Scheel, was custom-built for a yachtsman who wanted a big boat for daysails with crowds of friends.

and a navigator's station below decks for occasional overnights. The twenty-eight-foot (8.5m) *Grimalkin* is based on a sharpie yacht named *Egret* that was designed in the 1880s by Commodore Ralph Munroe. The commodore was one of the pioneer settlers of Miami, and his elegant centerboard sharpies, with two gaff-headed sails on unstayed masts—cat ketches—became a local fleet on Biscayne Bay more than a hundred years ago. They are stilll admired for their good looks, their simplicity, their shallow draft with the centerboard raised, and their amazing ability to sail through disturbed water with control if not comfort. Commodore Munroe regularly ran wild Florida inlets in *Egret*.

True to her name, *Patrician* is less of a daredevil. She was designed by Henry Scheel with the gentle, graceful, unostentatious lines of 1940s and 1950s cruiser-racers. This is an aesthetic that is, in fact, patrician. As a day boat, this fifty-five-foot (16.7m) sloop is beyond the upper limits of the type. Most day boats are less than thirty feet (9.1m). But the owner wanted what he considered "the perfect daysailer," a boat that could be sailed by one person, could accommodate a number of guests, would handle with the feel of a big boat, and would have presence. *Patrician* definitely has presence. Van Dam Wood Craft of Harbor Springs, Michigan, built her with perfectly fitted expanses and nuances of teak and mahogany, as the photos in these pages show. The shop also engineered and built the hydraulic and electrical systems that enable all lines and controls to be managed from the helm station with its big stainless-steel wheel.

Daysailers as large and as sophisticated as *Patrician* are very rare, but their size and their systems are inspired by the same day boat idea as the simple hull and single sail of a Beetle Cat. The idea is to get out on the water and into the weather for fun, for a modest adventure down the coast or around the bend, for an excursion whose purpose is not much more than being there—and that can be a lot.

Note: Sources for plans, patterns, kits, and completed boats can be found at the back of this book.

Cruising Classics

SAILING ACROSS OCEANS IN SMALL BOATS IS NOW A HUNDRED YEARS OLD AS A FEAT, A SPORT, AND FOR SOME A LIFESTYLE. ALTHOUGH SMALL BOATS CARRIED SETTLERS, ADVENTURERS, AND IN SOME CASES HAP- LESS MARINERS BLOWN OFF COURSE ACROSS WIDE STRETCHES OF WATER IN THE DIMMEST PAST, AND THE SAILORS OF THE PACIFIC TRADED and visited in small boats all over their island world, it was Joshua Slocum who showed modern cruising sailors what was possible.

A native of Nova Scotia, Slocum had spent thirty-five years at sea aboard small tramping and coasting vessels—schooners and barks—and one full-rigged ship of two thousand tons (1,814t). His voyages as seaman, mate, and master had taken him to China, Japan, Alaska, Australia, the Philippines, Brazil, Argentina, England, Ireland, and ports up and down both coasts of the United States and Canada. He was a master mariner familiar with the winds, seas, and coasts of much of the world in the 1890s. And in the 1890s, in the last decades of sail, he was on the beach and unemployed.

Slocum had already done something remarkable with a small boat. In 1887, with his family living aboard the small bark *Aquidneck*, which was 140 feet (42.5m) on deck, Slocum took the vessel to Paranaguá, Brazil, to load timber. With a full cargo she headed for sea, but in the broad Bay of Paranaguá she stuck fast on a sandbar and proceeded to pound herself to pieces. Slocum set to work to build a thirty-five-foot (10.5m) dory-style boat he called *Liberdade* from pieces of *Aquidneck*, and he rigged her with three Chinese-style lugsails battened with bamboo. With his family aboard, he sailed this "canoe," as he called it, from Brazil to South Carolina—fifty-five hundred miles (8,850km) in fifty-three sailing days.

A muscular cruising boat capable of traveling anywhere on the world's oceans, the thirty-five-foot (10.7m) *Zulu* has a traditional gaff-headed yawl rig on strong spars and rigging.

"It required confidence and some courage to face the first storm in so small a bark, after having been many years in large ships," he later wrote of the *Liberdade* adventure. Then he added that "the old boating trick came back fresh to me, the love of the thing itself."

The boating trick that made Slocum world-famous was sailing alone around the world between 1895 and 1898 by way of the Straits of Magellan at the tip of South America and the Cape of Good Hope at the bottom of Africa. This first voyage around the world by a lone human being was done aboard a former thirty-seven-foot (11.2m) fishing boat that Slocum rebuilt while he was out of work in Fairhaven, Massachusetts. His *Spray* was a fishing-smack type, a gaff-rigged sloop to which he added a lug-rigged mizzen all the way aft, making her a yawl. When his charming book about the adventure, *Sailing Alone Around the World*, was published in 1900, it was a bestseller. The book is still in print.

THE ART OF CRUISING

Among the simple pleasures of cruising are admiring the sunset from a safe anchorage, as below, and unhurried sailing on a blue-sky day, as the little schooner is doing on the opposite page.

Today there are as many as five thousand cruising sailboats on the world's oceans, some following *Spray*'s track around the world, others making shorter passages on courses that have become so standard in the world of ocean cruising that they are sometimes called "milk runs"—France to the West Indies, San Diego to Hawaii, the Panama Canal to the Galapagos and on to Tahiti. A hundred years ago it was believed by everyone, and perhaps especially by master mariners like Joshua Slocum, that ships went to sea and boats stayed within sight of land. Slocum indicated the distinction, but he wrote of "the love of the thing itself"—handling a small boat at sea or alongshore, keeping an eye on the weather, sailing all afternoon on a reach in a steady wind with no alteration of course or sail trim, and, late in the day, being just where you hoped to be when you studied the chart in the morning.

To be cruising is to be in continuous touch with the thing itself. Cruising is living aboard the boat for a long weekend, a week, a month, or a season, and sailing in to new harbors, along new coasts—having an adventure. Ocean-cruising sailors can spend years on such adventures, as Slocum did, but the pleasures and responsibilities of the thing itself are the same for a weekend cruise to visit friends down the bay as for a passage from England to the Azores. There is nothing like being master of your own little floating home, a vehicle where you live, play, get serious about such things as navigation and gear maintenance, and above all travel in a style that is wholly different from every form of travel on land. It is also greater in its possibilities than any form of land travel. Except for landlocked lakes, every waterway on the globe is connected to every other. A sailor on the Ohio River in Cincinnati could—if one had the boat, the time, and the skills—cruise to Canton on the Pearl River in China or visit nearly anywhere else he or she chose on the world's oceans and rivers. The sea's broad highway has unlimited exits and entrances.

Freedom of movement is only one of the unique freedoms of cruising, whether the trip is up the coast or around the world. There is a palpable release from the land—colloquially, a "sea change"—that lets you know you are somewhere else when you're cruising. And you *are* somewhere else. You are in that other world of water, at home in your own floating household, messy as it might be. The world, or at least the part an oyster would understand, is your oyster.

SOME CLASSIC CRUISING BOATS

Boats for cruising need not be large, and in fact a nimble little boat with a place for everything (but maybe not very much) and with everything in its place can have its charms. A perfect example is a design that S.S. Crocker called Sallee Rover, a twenty-foot (6m) sloop or yawl with a clipper-style profile based on the sloop boats of the nineteenth century. In this little cruiser are two seat berths flanking a big centerboard, but there is no head or galley, although miniature accommodations for both are possible. This is a boat for camping-out cruising in the style of the English canoe-yawl sailors of the 1890s. Sallee Rover plans are available from the WoodenBoat Store in Maine, some of whose employees are admirers of a local sloop built to those plans that is part of the harborscape.

Another classic small cruising package is a muscular twenty-four-foot (7.3m) yawl created by legendary catboat designer Fenwick Williams in 1932: a double-ended keelboat with fishing-vessel ancestry and with more hull volume than most little yachts of her length. This is an offshore-cruising vehicle for one or two sailors that has heavy construction, a displacement of nine thousand pounds (4t), good behavior at sea, and overnight accommodations for four, plus a tiny galley and portable head. Plans for this miniature blue-water cruiser, designed for carvel construction in wood, are published by the WoodenBoat Store.

Like the Williams yawl, William Garden's design for a double-ended cat schooner of generous proportions and scantlings is a bigger boat than its measurements—twenty-seven feet (8.2m) on deck, ten-foot (3m) beam, and four-foot (1.2m) draft—would indicate. *Itatae*, a boat built to this design, is a good example of how much big-boat feel and real usefulness—not to mention style—have been contrived and built into this little coastal cruiser. The two long seats that flank the folding table double as berths; the table has a built-in wine cooler; the galley has a real little cast-iron stove; and a tiny water closet is concealed under a hatch forward. But everything on *Itatae* is miniaturized, including headroom, which is five feet six inches (1.6m) under the closed companionway hatch. Nevertheless, it would be a pleasure for someone six feet (1.8m) tall to sit or crouch in such a space,

Built as a cruising yacht, then renowned as a racing yacht, and now a cruising yacht again, *Ticonderoga* is a legend in the sailing world for her power and beauty, down to the gilded dolphins that decorate her sheerline.

perhaps especially at anchor with a roast reaching perfection in the cookstove and guests enjoying wine and cheese around the little table.

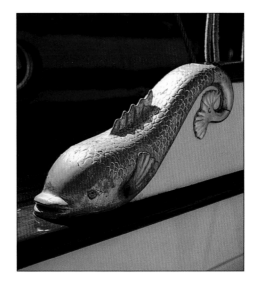

All of L. Francis Herreshoff's designs for small cruising sailboats are classics, and two of them are worthy of note here: one a cruising keelboat less than thirty feet (9.1m) with basic overnight amenities, the other a thirty-six-foot (11m) clipper-style yacht with greater space for people, gear, and stores. The H-28—with twenty-eight-foot-by-eight-foot-nine-inch (8.5 by 2.6m) beam and three-foot-six-inch (1m) draft—is a little cruising boat with comfortable accommodations for two below decks, an easily managed ketch rig, a transom-hung rudder that steers with a tiller, and good behavior at sea with twenty-eight hundred pounds (1,271kg) of lead more than three feet (91.5cm) down at the bottom of her keel. One careful critic of small-yacht design has called the H-28 "an original essence of a small cruising boat"—in other words, a classic—an accurate description of a twenty-eight-foot (8.5m) keelboat that can travel comfortably and safely off soundings or alongshore.

Herreshoff's Nereia design—thirty-six feet (11m) with eleven-foot (3.3m) beam and five-foot-three-inch (1.6m) draft—is a boat the designer described as "a real little ship," a bigger version of the H-28 and something of a half-size version of Herreshoff's legendary cruising-racing masterpiece, *Ticonderoga.* The Nereia design has room below for two seat berths flanking a folding table, two vee berths forward, moderate head and galley fixtures, good stowage, and above all great style, with her raked masts, wineglass transom, artistic curve of sheerline, and bowsprit with trailboards. This is a clipper yacht inspired by the clipper schooners of nineteenth-century yachting, not the clipper-style workboats that the Sallee Rover design resembles. Both the H-28 and the Nereia design are built to order with fiberglass hulls by Middleton Marine in Florida. Both are head-turners.

Other cruising head-turners on waterfronts dominated by useful, dependable, unremarkable fiberglass boats for cruising and daysailing are Lester Rosenblatt's *Rosa II*, a forty-one-foot (12.5m) ketch, and *Malabar II*, a forty-one-foot (12.5m) Alden schooner. *Rosa II* is one of the most beautiful sailboats in America—clipper bow complemented by a long stern overhang, sheerline curve subtly repeated by a line in relief where a cove stripe might be on an ordinary yacht, perfect proportions of hull and house and rig, and varnish like plate glass. The Rosenblatts have been big-ship naval architects for most of the twentieth century, and the family firm has produced relatively few designs for yachts. The second *Rosa*, successor to a thirty-foot (9.1m) clipper-style ketch, was codesigned by Lester Rosenblatt and his father, Mandell, and built by Paul Luke in Maine in 1959–60. She cruises the U.S. and Canadian East Coast from May to October, and from Nova Scotia to Virginia she provides everyone who sees her with the correct definition of a classic.

A classic cruising boat today. John Alden's second *Malabar* was an ocean racer in the 1920s, a yacht based on the capable fishing schooners of New England.

A modern cruising classic, with fiberglass hull and varnished wood on deck and below, is the Hinckley Sou'wester 42.

In America, "Alden schooner" is a generic term on the yachting waterfront. John Alden's Boston design firm produced drawings for 170 schooner yachts from the 1920s into the 1960s, basing most of them on the North Atlantic fishing schooners of the late nineteenth and early twentieth centuries, and designing them to race as well as cruise in that era from the 1920s through the 1950s when the ocean-racing rules encouraged the compatibility of racing and cruising. *Malabar II*, built in 1922 and raced successfully in her first season by Alden himself, was the second of Alden's influential designs for cruising boats that could race and racing boats that could comfortably cruise. She's a characteristic Alden schooner, with spoon bow and bowsprit, fishing-schooner sheerline, not a lot of varnish or fanciness, in keeping with her workboat inspiration, a businesslike gaff-schooner rig, and dark hull paint just like, in fact, a fishing schooner. *Malabar II* now cruises New England in summer and races in several classic yacht regattas that have come along in recent years as celebrations of sailing classics and as gatherings of the faithful.

The revival of ocean racing after World War II brought with it larger fleets with smaller boats, generally between thirty-six and sixty feet (11 and 18.2m), and a type that was not new but would reach a state of perfection during the 1950s—the cruiser-racer that could join a racing fleet or take a family on a comfortable extended vacation on the water. Yacht designers on both sides of the Atlantic produced classic cruising-racing sloops, yawls, and ketches that, no longer competitive, are now strictly cruising boats. Although occasional new boats of the type are built in wood, most cruising-racing yachts with the lines of the 1950s classics are now fiberglass with varnished mahogany or teak trim. They are elite boats.

An especially elite example is the Hinckley Sou'wester 42, built since 1982 to a design by Jim McCurdy and described by the Hinckley Company as "a solid, safe offshore yacht." Hinckley is a

Perhaps the most successful of the cruising-racing yachts that came along after World War II were the Concordias, in thirty-nine (11.9m) and forty-one foot (12.3m) lengths, and with sloop or yawl rigs. The trademark star at the bow is matched by a crescent moon at the stern.

Rolls-Royce kind of company, and all of its cruising boats, from forty-two to seventy feet (12.8 to 21.3m), share the classic cruiser-racer aesthetic: bladelike bow, small amount of overhang aft finished off with a shapely transom, low and small-windowed house structures that fair neatly into teak-capped bulwarks or coamings around the cockpit, and businesslike rig and fittings. To this the Hinckley Company adds the luxury of select teak and Honduras mahogany in such details as the cockpit's folding table, trim around the hatches and companionway, and furnishings below decks.

Catboats are classic cruising sailboats in the United States for two big reasons and possibly a lot of little ones. They are very beamy and thus very roomy below decks compared with other cruising machines, and they are throwbacks to the nineteenth-century waterfront of big gaff sails and sculptural hull forms. In their chubby and poky way they are beautiful, and as cruising vehi-

cles they are unsurpassed for accommodation possibilities in a small package. Few catboats are bigger than thirty feet (9.1m) on deck, and it is typical for a twenty-five-footer (7.6m) to have two big berths, a head compartment with shower, a dining table capable of serving six, a galley with a real range instead of a two-burner alcohol stove, and an auxiliary engine for locomotion when the wind is not cooperative and to charge a bank of batteries. Cruising catboats, like motorsailers, have never been numerous in sailing's fleet of more conventional types, but they have had loyal cruising partisans, inspired designers, and careful builders for most of the twentieth century.

Motorsailers, as the name suggests, are cruising sailboats that have equal capabilities of comfort and passage-making under sail or power. Depending upon hull form and size of engine, they can be cruising powerboats that happen to have sails or cruising sailboats that have big engines. Either way they are more commodious—more "houseboaty"—than conventional cruising sailboats, which generally have the style and volume of postwar cruiser-racers. A motorsailer's sails are there for progress under sail, although speed is not a consideration, and also for their steadying effect at sea. The engine is there for good long runs when the wind is absent or fluky and to power into port in bad weather.

Two good examples of motorsailers are the fiberglass Nauticats built in Finland and *Burma*, a big fifty-eight-foot (17.6m) cutter designed by R.O. Davis, who carried on the motorsailer tradition begun by the celebrated William Hand, in whose design office Davis worked as a designer-draftsman for twenty years. Hand virtually invented the motorsailer as a type in the 1920s, combining the diesel engines that were proving their worth in workboats and fishing boats with the hulls and rigs of workboat-style cruising yachts. Hand's first motorsailers looked like fishing vessels converted for cruising, but they soon got sleeker while keeping the seaworthiness and heavy construction of their commercial inspiration. Davis' *Burma*, designed in the late 1940s and launched in 1950, has great yacht style as well as motorsailer roominess, comfort, and ability at sea.

The Nauticats, popular all over the world, are similar exercises in combining hulls of fairly large volume with modern, ultra-reliable diesel engines and a sailplan big enough to push the package with a sense of being under sail. The Nauticat 52 has a tall ketch rig with big cutter-style headsails, all accompanied by strong spars, fittings, and rigging. This is a yacht for offshore cruising. As with *Burma*, a big pilothouse amidships is a motorsailer characteristic, with the difference that *Burma*, which is built of wood, has very little obvious wood showing and the Nauticat, which is fiberglass, has rails, trim, and other details of varnished teak. Both boats have raw teak decks for best possible footing in wet conditions. Below decks the Nauticat 52 has furnishings and bulkheads of varnished teak in a layout that provides quarters for as many as ten. The Nauticats are semicustom boats with a choice of interior arrangements and possibilities, including that Finnish necessity, a sauna.

Joshua Slocum's *Spray*, despite workboat ancestry and rebuilding by a deep-water-sailing veteran, was not as safe or substantial an offshore cruiser as the old skipper might have sailed around the world had he been given a choice. One choice for ocean adventuring from Slocum's time until our own has been a heavily built and deep-keeled double-ender based on the pilot boats and offshore

Burma **is a classic American motorsailer— brawny, roomy, and capable of motoring or sailing through any weather to stay on schedule.**

rescue vessels designed by Colin Archer in the late nineteenth and early twentieth centuries. These slow-sailing but very able and predictable boats, from thirty feet (9.1m) to not more than fifty feet (15.2m), designed for Norway, where Archer's family had emigrated from Scotland, became legends in the sailing world. Yachts based on them were designed by Archer himself and by naval architects in the United States, notably John Hanna, whose Tahiti ketch became as generic as the Alden schooner, and William Atkin, whose wonderful Archer-inspired offshore yachts had Scandinavian design names like Eric and Ingrid.

A recent offshore-cruising boat in both the Slocum and Archer traditions is *Zulu*, a thirty-five-foot (10.5m) gaff-rigged yawl with bowsprit and boomkin, husky workboat-style hull, and inspiration from a number of directions, including Harry Pidgeon's *Islander*, which that successor to Slocum sailed twice around the world. Another inspiration is Slocum's old *Spray*. The difference with *Zulu* is that she's significantly prettier than *Spray* or *Islander* and has the deeper keel and greater ballast that made the Archer double-enders so well behaved and tractable at sea. *Zulu* was designed by the couple that own and sail her. George and Julia Maynard also built her. It took them six years of winter labor to create this classic, brawny ocean-cruising boat from select wood and other good material acquired or made. They now live aboard *Zulu* in Port Townsend, Washington, and cruise whenever they like. Money and time permitting, the Maynards can go wherever they like in a home and vehicle like *Zulu*.

Zulu exemplifies the classic husky cruising boat able to deliver her people anywhere on the world's oceans. The little Sallee Rover sloop represents cruising as a basic getaway with minimum accommodations and close-to-shore capabilities. What they both share is the sense and the reality of a home on the water, a vehicle whose recreational possibilities can range from anchoring in a little bay where there's nobody else within sight or sound to tying up in a crowded marina where the locals are friendly and the nightlife is something to write home about—and, it might be added, where the friendly locals and the resident cruising types will envy your floating home if it's a classic.

Note: Sources for plans, patterns, kits, and completed boats can be found at the back of this book.

Cruising boats are floating homes as well as vehicles for sailing over the horizon. This is *Zulu*'s very homey main cabin.

Chapter Five

SAILBOAT RACING IS ONE OF THE WORLD'S POPULAR COMPETITIVE SPORTS—NOT AS EVERYDAY AS GOLF OR TENNIS, NOT AS ATHLETIC AS RUNNING OR SOCCER, AND NOT AS EASY TO ADOPT AS ANY OF THESE. FOR SAILBOAT RACING YOU NEED A BOAT—AND NOT JUST ANY BOAT. IT MUST BE A RACING BOAT, OR AT LEAST A BOAT accepted for racing by any number of controlling organizations in the sport. More often than not, it must be a racing boat that conforms to the measurements and other requirements of a one-design class or sponsoring/governing organization. All of this is necessary for the same reasons that family cars are not eligible to compete at LeMans or Indianapolis.

The rules and measurements ensure that the racing activity is orderly and theoretically fair, and that none of the boats are freaks intended to humble the rest of the fleet with some design or mechanical advantage. In one-design classes the boats in competition are the same within rigid parameters of considerations like weight, sail area, and hull dimensions, although there are development classes whose rules encourage modest innovation and permit boats that have some differences.

Racing classics come in a variety of types and sizes. The common denominator is the excitement of getting boat, gear, and crew up to speed and staying there, as this spinnaker-flying sloop seems to be doing.

ONE-DESIGN CLASSICS

The United States Sailing Association (USSA) lists 140 active one-design classes in its 1997 directory. There are many others elsewhere in the world, some of them the same classes in their own national organizations, and there are local or national boats developed by clubs or boatbuilders that compete, say, only in Sweden or New Zealand. One such U.S. class, a yacht-club one-design class that only races in its home waters, is the Wianno Senior, first designed and built for the Wianno Yacht Club of Cape Cod in 1913. Still very active, the fleet has recently been augmented with new fiberglass boats that match the old wood boats in everything including stiffness and weight. This twenty-five-foot (7.6m) day racer with old-fashioned gaff rig is an amazing survivor among all the club boats that were designed and built to bring evenhanded racing to one group of sailors. Of the 160 wooden Wiannos built between 1913 and 1976, an estimated 130 are still around, if not still racing. One of them is *Victura*, John F. Kennedy's Wianno Senior, now on display at the John F. Kennedy Library in Boston.

Other one-design classes not listed in the USSA directory are survivors of the International Rule and Universal Rule classes established early in the twentieth century, when sailboat racing in the United States and Europe had become enough of a phenomenon to call for rules and rule-making organizations.

Even ocean racing in boats bigger than thirty feet (9.1m) has had rules for most of the twentieth century. Ocean racing is more than an organized start from one port and a timed finish at another—for example, from Newport, Rhode Island, to Hamilton, Bermuda. It is also an exercise in handicapping all the boats in the fleet so that each one races level with every other. This has never been easy, and the history of yacht racing and racing-yacht design has been to some extent a history of rules and measurement formulas changing with new boats, new conditions, and the crafty work of naval architects designing yachts that can sail through loopholes in the rules. Ocean racing also requires safety rules, construction rules, and crew-experience rules in a sport that is dangerous.

Two of the early rule-making attempts were the Universal Rule devised by Nathanael Herreshoff, then the world's most successful yacht designer, in 1903, and the International Rule developed in Europe in 1906. The Universal Rule

A classic Wianno Senior one-design blasts through a lump of sea in a shower of spray during the annual Opera House Cup Race at Nantucket, off the coast of Cape Cod.

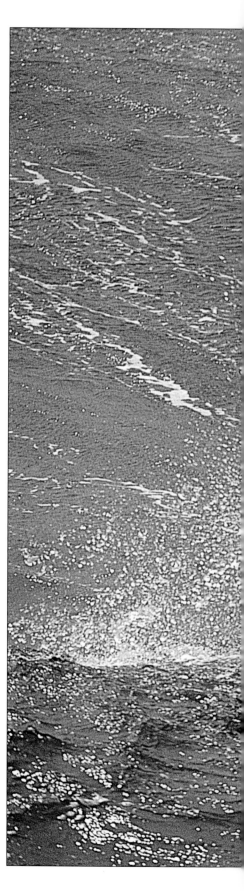

divided racing yachts into classes according to size, and gave each a letter of the alphabet. The most famous of these were the J-class yachts of roughly 80-foot (24.3m) waterline length and 130-foot (39.6m) overall length that raced for the America's Cup in the 1930s. The International Rule also sorted racing yachts into classes according to size, and gave each a number of meters as a designation that did not describe the boat's size but was instead the result of a complicated formula. The most famous of these are the 12-meters that competed for the America's Cup from the 1950s to the 1980s. They are generally 65 to 70 feet (19.8 to 21.3m) in overall length—much more than 12 meters long—but their complex of hull and sail measurements will come out at 12 meters when all the design scheming is done. There are also square-meter classes—40-square-meter, 30-square-meter, 22-square-meter—that were developed in Scandinavia with completely different rules and math. If that isn't confusing enough, if a J-boat or a 12-meter were to go ocean racing, the formula for handicapping the boat would involve completely different calculations. Perhaps fortunately, Js and 12s are not meant to race offshore.

Two significant survivors from the early days of rule-making are the Herreshoff S-boats and the several meter classes that still race in the United States and Europe. The S-boats are an active racing fleet of antiques with centers of activity on Narragansett Bay, where they were built by the Herreshoffs, and on Long Island, New York. The Herreshoff Manufacturing Company built ninety-six S-boats between 1919 and 1941, and it is thought that as many as fifty of them are still around. The S-boat is an attractive twenty-seven-foot-six-inch (8.3m) day racer similar to the yacht-club boats that came along from the 1880s to the 1920s, a lively performer and a status item among admirers of antique sailboats.

The most active of the meter boats are the 6-meters, a development class that tends to attract owners technical enough to enjoy the creative exercise of trying for a better 6 and rich enough to pay for a custom-designed and custom-built thirty-six-foot (11m) boat that may be made of epoxy-

OPPOSITE: A classic Herreshoff S-boat buries her lee rail under the press of her sails and a brisk wind blowing from the side—a beam reach, the fastest point of sail for most keelboats. ABOVE: A gathering of 6-meter boats ready for a race.

molded wood and look like a floating Stradivarius. Of the meter classes, the 8-, 6-, and 5.5-meter classes are most active. The surviving 12-meters are antiques—or at least boats left over from the last America's Cup campaigns sailed in 12s during the 1970s and 1980s—that now compete in classic yacht regattas and keep alive the glory they once knew as the most competitive of the International Rule boats in the United States and Europe during the 1920s and 1930s.

A racing classic that is making a comeback in replica form—and to some extent as inspiration for new classes of all-out no-rules sailboat racing all over the world—is the old sandbagger of the last half of the nineteenth century in the United States. Sandbagger racing, with its few rules, no restrictions on the amount of sail no matter how small the boat, and perhaps more subtly its crews of sailing roughnecks, was one of the reasons for the rule-making that came to sailboat racing at the beginning of the twentieth century in the United States.

Nevertheless, rule-making has never completely defeated fun and daring, and boats that race with few rules, much sail, and a certain rowdiness have returned. A few of them, like Australia's Sydney 18s, never went away. Today, replica Sandbaggers built by the Independence Seaport Museum in Philadelphia are used for exhibition racing, for teamwork programs, and simply to see a racing classic sail again. Only a handful of the sandbaggers built more than a hundred years ago are still intact, and most of those are in museums.

Another classic that has never gone away, and another extreme type, is the racing scow. Beamy and flat-bottomed like the sandbaggers, the scows that raced a hundred years ago for such trophies as the Seawanhaka Cup were further evidence that order needed to be restored. But the shaping up of sailing in Europe and on the U.S. East Coast was ignored by scow sailors. Several classes of scows, shooting along under too much sail and close to capsizing, have been active on the lakes of the U.S. Midwest for generations.

A final example of good old too-much-sail, frantic-athleticism, local-color sailing is the fleet of log canoes that race every summer on Chesapeake Bay. These boats are classics not only for their lively and even theatrical performances and lovely clipper aesthetics, but for the fact that they are made from logs sculpted and pinned together. The dugout canoes of Virginia's Indians were their distant ancestors.

The one-design classes that came along in sailboat racing from the 1920s through the 1960s were mostly more sedate creations, intended as boats for families to sail for uncompetitive recreation and as boats to race in yacht-club competition. Many were also intended for construction in the family garage or workshop, an idea that mass-production fiberglass boatbuilding has compromised if not killed altogether. Stars, Comets, Lightnings, and Snipes are familiar racing one-designs, and the Star is literally the star of the fleet—raced all over the world for eighty years. Perhaps the most competitive of all the one-design classes, the Star has been the apprenticeship for some of the world's great racing sailors.

An early classic one-design active on both sides of the Atlantic since the 1920s, the International 14 is the prototype for all the racing-dinghy classes active in the world today. An

English-dinghy type, the International 14 was originally built in wood, all curves and flashing varnish. A restored one is owned, not surprisingly, by the North American distributors of Epifanes yacht varnish, reputed to be the world's best. Modern International 14s are more angular, made of fiberglass, and equipped with aluminum spars and the latest go-fast fittings of stainless steel. They look somewhat industrial compared with the old wooden 14s, but they represent an accumulation of many experiments and improvements in this important little development class. As the great British yacht designer Uffa Fox wrote of them, "The International 14-foot [4.2m] dinghy is the father and mother of all our present-day drop-keel racers.... New shapes of hull, masting, rigging, sails, winches, and various gadgets, together with new techniques in sailing and handling, were all developed in these 14-footers."

Two larger one-design classes that have been legends since they began racing in the late 1920s are the Atlantic and the Dragon, both elegant fast keelboats for three crew, and both examples of designs that came along when sailing rigs were changing from the old gaff-headed sails and shorter masts of the nineteenth century to tall triangles of sail—the Marconi rig named for the radio aerials its masts and standing rigging resembled. The thirty-foot (9.1m) Atlantic, designed in 1927 by W.

True to their name, the International One-Designs established fleets in Europe and America after World War II and are still an active class.

Starling Burgess, is a U.S. class. The twenty-nine-foot (8.8m) Dragon, designed in 1928 by Norway's Johan Anker, is largely a European class. Perhaps the most famous Dragon in the world is *Bluebottle*, owned by the British royal family and raced by Prince Philip. Both classes are still active, although a majority of their fleets have fiberglass hulls today.

Bigger than Dragons and Atlantics, and representing the same new aerodynamic rigging technology and an even wider orbit of international racing, are two classic one-design boats that originated in Scandinavia: the 30-square-meter class, a slim forty-foot (12.1m) boat typical of Sweden's racing skerry cruisers and a result of the square-meter rule established in Sweden in 1908, and the thirty-three-foot-five-inch (10.1m) International One-Design, whose lines were drawn in 1936 by Bjarne Aas of Denmark. Both boats have small crouching-headroom cabins, although cruising was never their purpose. *Oriole II*, the 30-square-meter shown here, was designed by L. Francis Herreshoff and launched in 1930 for Sis Hovey of Boston. Hovey raced this boat in Sweden in 1930 as the first woman skipper in an international race and won her class in competition with 30-squares from Scandinavia and Germany that were sailed by people more experienced in this Baltic boat.

True to its name, the International One-Design (IOD) was raced all over the world after World War II, with especially active fleets in Bermuda, in Scandinavia, and on Long Island Sound in the United States. This is still an active class in all those places, and like the Star, the IOD has been a boat in which some of the world's great sailors perfected their skills, many of them for the big leagues of ocean racing.

OCEAN-RACING CLASSICS

Ocean racing, as compared with most one-design racing, is done in boats bigger than thirty-six feet (11m) and of great design and construction variety. There are several ocean-racing rules in the world of offshore competition that attempt to ensure the safety of the fleet, the integrity of the boats, the skills of the crews, and above all the fairness of a contest in which a factory-built thirty-six-footer (11m) may be racing against a custom-built seventy-footer (21.3m). The seventy-footer (21.3m) will be faster, custom-built or not, since sailing speed is greatly enhanced by a boat's waterline length and ability to carry sail. A longer boat with a lot of sail will always beat a shorter boat with less sail. But the rating (handicapping) rules of ocean racing attempt to level the playing field, never perfectly but sometimes with the result that the custom-built seventy-footer (21.3m) finishes first in fleet but the factory-built thirty-six-footer (11m) wins the race on "corrected time." Such things happen. What happens in reality and in the complexities of establishing ratings for handicapping is that the big boats give up increments of time to the smaller boats, and if a smaller boat finishes within the envelope of time it is allowed by the bigger end of the fleet, it wins.

Ocean racing is a different, difficult, demanding, and, it may as well be noted, expensive portion of a sport-sailing spectrum that runs from sailboards to big boats with full crews of athletes sailing around the world. In the seventy-odd years since modern ocean racing began in the United States and Europe, there have been many classic competitors and breakthrough designs, for ocean racing represents the ultimate development class. Perhaps no other ocean racer had more success in her first seasons or represented a greater breakthrough than *Dorade,* the slim, fifty-two-foot-by-ten-foot-three-inch (15.8 by 3.1m) yawl designed by Olin Stephens at the beginning of his career. *Dorade* was designed and built for Olin's father, Roderick Stephens, Sr., and sailed by his two sons, Olin and Rod Jr. In the 1931 season *Dorade* won the transatlantic race from Newport, Rhode Island, to Plymouth, England, in seventeen days, arriving two full days before the rest of the fleet. Then she won Britain's prestigious Fastnet Race against sixteen other yachts from England, America, and France. She won the Fastnet again in 1933.

Dorade began the remarkable yacht-design career of Olin Stephens and influenced the cruising-racing type that came along in ocean racing in the 1930s, displacing the Alden schooners that had been the favored vessels for cruising and racing offshore during the 1920s in the United States. *Dorade*'s heirs are many, and many of them are classics, but one worthy of mention here is *Dorade*'s successor, *Stormy Weather*, launched for Olin's brother in 1934. *Stormy Weather*—fifty-four feet by twelve feet six inches (16.4 by 3.8m)—was an improved *Dorade*, and as if to prove it she won a transatlantic race from Newport, Rhode Island, to Bergen, Norway, in 1935, and that year won Britain's Fastnet Race, a third straight Fastnet victory for the Stephens brothers.

Racing sailboats, contrasted with cruising sailboats and boats whose sailing is just fooling around, have a certain élan. They are often, oddly enough, racy. And like romantic heroes and heroines they tend to die young. Once its competitive life is over or the class goes into decline, a racing sailboat can spend the rest of its life as a resource for rot, full of wet leaves behind the clubhouse or filled with dirt and planted with petunias. Even ocean-racing boats can have a declining history as cruising boats that aren't quite right. Yes, the owner tells you as he chips the already lifting paint from the once-varnished house of an old ocean racer, this boat won Class C in the Marblehead–Halifax Race in 1960. Then he tells you that he and the family don't sail it much because it leaks a lot and isn't easy to handle.

But depending upon your definition of a classic—in general the best and most enduring of any object or type, from neckties to suspension bridges—you could decide that most racing sailboats are classics. The boats considered here are certainly among the best and most enduring of their type, and most are from the hand-built, wooden era. There are many racing classics in the world of sailing—wood and fiberglass, derelict and gleaming, winners and losers. Some of them were launched just today.

Note: Sources for plans, patterns, kits, and completed boats can be found at the back of this book.

Dorade, the slim fifty-two-foot (15.8m) yawl designed by Olin Stephens in 1931, transformed the world of ocean racing in the l930s. She was sailed in her first seasons by Olin and Rod Stephens.

Replicas and Reinterpretations

SAILING'S PAST IS SO HISTORICALLY, SOCIALLY, AND TECHNICALLY INTERESTING THAT MANY SAILORS HAVE DECIDED TO STOP RIGHT THERE—AT THE CANOE-YAWL ERA OF ADVENTUROUS SMALL-YACHT SAILING IN THE 1890s IN ENGLAND, FOR EXAMPLE, OR AT THE FRIENDSHIP SLOOP ERA OF GRACEFUL SMALL FISHING BOATS

with clipper details, beam-as-ballast hull design, and weekend accommodations with oaken bucket. There are many other choices of racing and cruising sailboats that have the aesthetics and the indefinable atmosphere of little boats from the past and that in most cases deliver satisfying performance to match such ephemeral stuff. After all, old designs and old ideas of being on the water were developed over centuries, and satisfying performance—whether speed off the wind or predictable behavior or plenty of room down below—was of value for the fishermen and yachtsmen who used and shaped these boats in the past.

Replicas and reinterpretations are all about the past. They are about the promise of romance, perhaps, or some aesthetic truth they may deliver in contrast to the new plastic boats that seem to be designed by the same people who design refrigerators. Replicas and reinterpretations are all about performance in real terms: how hard is this boat to handle? How comfortable is it to spend a weekend aboard? How will I feel sailing this anachronism in the overwhelming fleet of modern boats? And how much work will it be to maintain? The answer to the second-to-last question is that you might feel like Henry David Thoreau, who thought his own company and opinions were just about right—and who probably would approve of your boat. The answer to the last question, in the replica and reinterpretation era of the 1980s and

Jarvis Newman's replica Friendship sloops are based on his own *Dictator,* **shown here.**

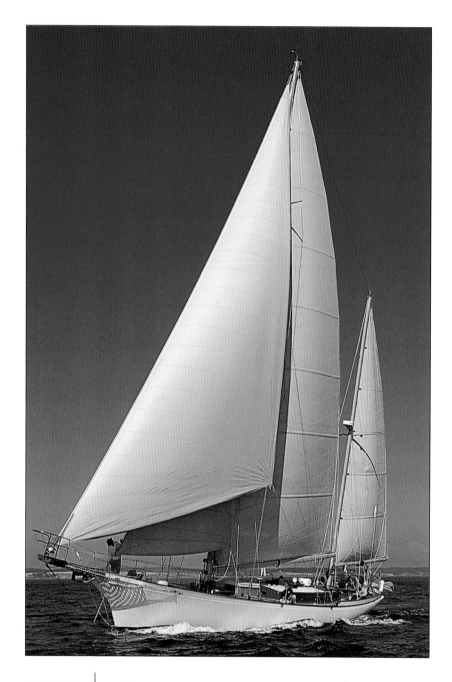

OPPOSITE: Many new copies of traditional small boats are built by amateurs from plans and kits. Shown under construction is a Western Skiff built from a kit from England's *Classic Boat* magazine. ABOVE: Replicas come in all sizes, types, and degrees of prestige. This is *Radiance*, a copy of the great *Ticonderoga*.

1990s, is that a new boat built to look and behave like an old boat will be a lot easier to maintain than the wooden boat it replicates or reinterprets. This is true even for new boats made of wood, thanks to epoxy resin and its preservation properties. And fiberglass, for all its aesthetic misuse in many new boats, is a material that can shape sturdy, dry, and even aesthetically pleasing hulls. Most fiberglass replicas and reinterpretations of boats from the past, with their traditional lines and varnished-wood details, cannot be picked out in a fleet of genuine antiques.

People may choose particular replicas and reinterpretations of old boats for practical reasons like upkeep, but they will first be attracted by their romance, practical considerations notwithstanding. The romance they find in these boats will be many things, "romance" being a word that covers a lot of territory. Some may discover the appeal of feeling the same tug of wind and vibration of tiller an Edwardian yachtsman would have felt on a brisk day. Others may enjoy suiting the boat to the place—sailing a fat Cape Cod catboat across Buzzards Bay to the Elizabeth Islands, for example, a trip that hundreds of her ancestors made a hundred years ago. More than anything else, the beauty of traditional small boats will attract sailors to their originals or their replicas. Traditional small boats have the fundamental wooden-boat beauty of things shaped by the limitations and liberties of what a clever person might make from a supply of wood. There have been many clever people in that game, all the way back to Noah, and from roughly 1800 to 1960 there were great small boats created by builders who worked in wood all over the world. These are the yachts and working types being re-created today, in new materials and in new ways. Whatever they're made from now, these boats retain the shapes and details that came to them simply because their models were made out of wood—with long sweeps of line with no abrupt curves, bow and stern rising higher than the wider middle, and pieces fitted together at interesting angles rather than blended into something slicker. Wooden boats are essentially and aesthetically different from fiberglass and metal boats, and even when reproduced in other materials an essence and an aesthetic is kept, or should be kept.

UPDATES OF THE CLASSICS

Some of the best of today's replicas and reinterpretations of classic sailboats are small, and some are available as kits for home construction. Magazines are among the kit-boat suppliers today, in contrast to the 1950s and 1960s, when plywood boat kits produced by mail-order houses in America and Europe introduced new enthusiasts to boating and boatbuilding. This was good for the sport and hobby then and since, and the magazines can be commended for carrying on what is now a fifty-year-old tradition. France's *Chasse-Marée* has kits for an elegant fifteen-foot (4.5m) sailing dory with jib and lug-rigged mainsail, along with plans for a dozen

other traditional small boats. England's *Classic Boat* sells a kit for the thirteen-foot-seven-inch (4.1m) Western Skiff, a round-form

lapstrake rowing and sailing boat loosely based on West Country models that has the brawny English-workboat look reinterpreted

in less-brawny plywood. *WoodenBoat* magazine in the United States has kits for the Shellback dinghy (discussed in chapter three)

and the seven-foot-seven-inch (2.3m) Nutshell, a shapely plywood pram. Both are clever takes on old types but not really replicas or

close reinterpretations of traditional boats. Nevertheless, these kits are good introductions to wooden boatbuilding and to an appre-

ciation of traditional small boats.

Some replicas and reinterpretations are attempts to bring back a worthy or even classic small sailboat. Some are attempts—of-

ten successful—to create something new that has the aesthetic appeal or sailing magic of a classic boat that may be gone irretrievably or gone in the sense of nobody building that model or design anymore. And some replicas and reinterpretations are nearly pure exercises in re-creating classic types and styles: designing and building a boat that seems to have history, aesthetics, structure, patina—all the characteristics of a genuine old sailboat—but is really brand-new, never seen before. We might call these designs inspirations rather than down-to-the-nailheads replicas or close reinterpretations of a boat that is old or classic.

Two good examples of this last approach are the twenty-foot (6m) cat-yawl that her designer, that wizard of Gloucester, Phil Bolger, and her Gloucester builder, Brad Story, call the Chebacco 20, and the twenty-nine-foot-six-inch (9m) Roxane, designed and built in England by Nigel Irens Design. Bolger and Story's Chebacco has taken the name of an eighteenth-century New England cat schooner, a type somewhat the same size but much heftier, in style a sailing ship's boat rather than a centerboard boat of the nineteenth century. The new Chebacco is a hybrid of Cape Cod catboat and English Channel canoe-yawl. It has the broad centerboard hull of the catboat, along with a substantial rudder on the

OPPOSITE: Western Skiff is an attractive lapstrake day boat offered in a build-it-yourself kit from *Classic Boat* magazine. BELOW: A near-perfect little boat, the Shellback dinghy shows off her saucy lines and tall lugsail rig.

transom and a big gaff mainsail on a mast in the eyes of the boat. Its English influence includes a mizzen all the way aft and a weekending cabin all the way forward. The truth is that, despite its lovely and historic look, there never was anything like this until it was drawn by Bolger and built by Story in seamless cold-molded wood. The Chebacco looks like a local type from a hundred years ago, and by all accounts delivers weekend-cruising comfort and fun sailing along with undeniable style.

The same might be said of the Roxane design, which has the tall, dramatic, lug-rigged sails of the old French fishing fleet. This weekending boat is also a cat-yawl with centerboard/daggerboard, but she's much heavier than the roughly one-thousand-pound (454kg) Chebacco. Roxane displaces more than sixty-six hundred pounds (2.9t) and stands up to her sail area very well in coastal cruising. Down below, in slightly crouching headroom, are a small vee berth forward, generous seat berths amidships flanking a folding table, galley space near the companionway, and even sink and water closet compartments forward. A 1990s update on an 1890s Breton lugger, the Roxane design is built in wood or fiberglass by England's Dartington Boatworks.

Another English update on something old is the Cornish Crabber 24—also built as the Cornish Cutter 24—a boat that is thirty feet (9.1m) overall and twenty-four feet six inches (7.4m) on deck with a twenty-foot-nine-inch (6.3m) waterline and that can be delivered with gaff rig and tanbark sails or in the cutter version with sails of cream-colored Terylene. Either way, this keelboat with straight stem and long bowsprit, low house structure, and nice curve of sheerline suggests the past: in gaff rig a little West Country fishing type, in cutter rig a little West Country fishing type converted to

OPPOSITE: Designed by England's Nigel Irens, the dramatic lug-rigged cat-yawl Roxane is a weekend cruiser inspired by French fishing boats of the nineteenth century. RIGHT: Phil Bolger and Brad Story's Chebacco 20 is another inspired weekend cruiser. This is the plywood version with cat-yawl rig.

a 1930s cruising yacht. Down below are berths for four, an enclosed head, and a small galley in quarters nicely made from fiberglass moldings and quantities of varnished teak. These attractive boats with wood used for trim and interior joinerwork and—in the case of the gaff-rigged Crabber—spruce spars are fiberglass reinterpretations of classic British small boats. They are only two of a fleet of similar reinterpreted boats from Cornish Crabbers Ltd in the old seacoast duchy of Cornwall, a fleet that includes twelve-, sixteen-, and seventeen-foot (3.6, 4.8, and 5.1m) daysailers with traditional rigs and looks, plus nineteen- and twenty-two-foot (5.7 and 6.7m) weekend cruisers.

Some U.S. examples of the same replication or reinterpretation of attractive boats from the past hundred years are the recreational Friendship sloops produced in fiberglass by Newman Marine in Maine and the Edey & Duff Stone Horse, an exact fiberglass copy of S.S. Crocker's classic cruising keelboat of 1931.

Edey & Duff call their twenty-three-foot-six-inch-by-eighteen-foot-four-inch-by-seven-foot-one-inch-by three-foot-six-inch (7.1 by 5.5 by 2.1 by 1m) Stone Horse "a superior small cruiser"—which she is and has been for more than seventy years. Crocker gave her very sweet lines complemented by a tall but unstressed cutter rig and a full ballasted keel to carry the sail and give her good windward performance for a cruising boat. The raised deck is especially successful, giving this minimum-size cruising boat a more generous cabin lit by six portlights, affording a flat nonskid surface for deck work, and gracing the boat's profile with three complementary lines—the flat deck line, the nice curve of sheerline where the dark hull joins the white raised deck, and the deep curve that defines the cockpit. The cockpit is eight feet (2.4m) long and self-bailing, and all the running rigging is on its forward bulkhead. The nonskid fiberglass on deck is made to look like old-time painted canvas. Traditional considerations extend below, where the space at the foot of the companionway is a galley with a two-burner stove, a small sink, a big top-loading icebox that features real ice, and a comfortable seat for the cook or for down-below time. The space here is only four

OPPOSITE: The Stone Horse is a graceful weekend cruiser designed in the 1930s by S.S. Crocker. She's been replicated in fiberglass by Edey & Duff. ABOVE: The Cornish Crabber 24 is a fiberglass reinterpretation of English coastal workboats adapted for cruising—a weekender with four berths below deck.

101

feet (1.2m) high, but very attractive. Forward is a large vee berth with a water closet hidden underneath, along with stowage bins. This is a boat for spirited weekend cruising and overnighting with the thought that though you might bump your head, it's a small price to pay for the beauty of the boat's sweeping lines and low profile.

Friendship sloops, named for the Maine village whose shops built the best of them, were vehicles for a variety of alongshore fisheries in Maine, principally lobstering, during the last half of the nineteenth century. Also known as Muscongus Bay sloops and Maine sloop boats, they were the local type of a clipper-influenced fishing sloop common from Bar Harbor to Boston. When gasoline engines came along at the beginning of the twentieth century, the sloops were largely abandoned in favor of gas-engine launches that made a fisherman's work simpler. The gas-engine launches evolved into the Maine lobsterboat, and the old sloops evolved into a favored type for conversion as little cruising yachts.

The reason why can be seen in Newman Marine's twenty-five- and thirty-one-foot (7.6 and 9.4m) replicas—a little clipper of a boat with elegant sweeping sheerline, clipper bow with trailboards, low cabin curved to complement the curves elsewhere, and big gaff sailplan with jib-and-mainsail. These are beautiful little boats in original and replica form, but yachtsmen are attracted by more than their aesthetics. The common size of the original sloops was twenty to thirty feet (6 to 9.1m), family-weekending and single-

The Cape Cod catboat reinterpreted in fiberglass for cruising sailors, the Marshall 22, right, has generous below-decks space for a couple. It also has charming period details like the bronze cat's-eye port, opposite.

handing size; the keelboat version of the type combined relative beaminess—as much as nine feet (2.7m) for a boat twenty-five feet (7.6m) across the deck—with enough hull volume to accommodate several berths, a galley area, some stowage, and a water closet. The originals were striking, ideal yachts, and the replicas carry on the tradition.

Another New England workboat that survives nicely at the end of the twentieth century, both converted for cruising and replicated as a little yacht, is the Cape Cod catboat, noted previously. Very beamy, very roomy, and usually very shallow-draft, the centerboard catboats of twenty to thirty feet (6 to 9.1m) that once harvested fish, scallops, and oysters in southern New England were ideal yachts. Over the last hundred-odd years many were converted to yacht service, and probably as many more were built to serve as yachts from the beginning. Marshall Marine's fiberglass replicas, in fifteen-foot-six-inch, eighteen-foot-two-inch, and twenty-two-foot (4.7, 5.5, and 6.7m) lengths, continue this tradition. The Marshall 22 is a good example of how much cruising comfort a catboat can fit into a twenty-two-foot (6.7m) hull: an eight-foot (2.4m) -square cockpit, a good little galley, two six-foot-four-inch (1.9m) berths, a concealed water closet, a cabin table that folds out from the centerboard trunk, a lot of stowage, an icebox under one of the cockpit seats, and even a hanging locker. This boat's beam is ten feet two inches (3m)—nearly half her length. Draft is only two feet (61cm) with the centerboard up. This wading-depth draft means escape from crowded channels and harbors while cruising,

OPPOSITE: A replica of Nathanael Herreshoff's own *Alerion* sails out of Newport, Rhode Island. ABOVE: Mast hoops aboard the replica schooner *America.*

and the great beam means uncommon roominess in the cockpit and below for such a small package. On the yachting waterfronts of the United States, catboats are always said to be having a revival. The truth is that the catboat revival has been going strong for something like a hundred years.

Some other traditional boats that have never gone away, now replicated or reinterpreted in fiberglass, are Nathanael Herreshoff's designs for a twelve-foot-six-inch (3.8m) -waterline "boy's boat," commonly known as the 12 ½; a little keelboat fifteen feet ten inches (4.8m) on deck; Captain Nat's slightly larger twenty-foot-nine-inch (6.3m) Fish class, capable of reinterpretation as an overnight cruiser; and the designer's own third *Alerion*, a twenty-six-foot (7.9m) sloop that must em-

body all the small-boat wisdom Nat Herreshoff accumulated in the sixty-four great years before he drew her lines. These are all elite little yachts in the Herreshoff tradition, and it is no surprise that they survive like Bugattis in real and replicated form.

The *Alerion* has been replicated by two builders—Rumery's Boat Yard in Maine and Alfred Sanford's shop in Nantucket. Both are faithful replicas of "the beautiful *Alerion*"—Rumery's in foam-core fiberglass with wood trim, Sanford's in veneers of wood cold-molded with epoxy. Both depart from Captain Nat's original daysailer, now restored and on display at Mystic Seaport, by being overnight cruising boats with berths and other conveniences in the little cabin.

The twenty-foot-nine-inch (6.3m) Fish, another day boat now replicated in an overnight-cruising version, is built by Connecticut's Noank Marine Service in largely original form with varnished-wood spars, washboards, seats, sheerstrakes, and cabin doors. This nicely disguises the fiberglass hull and deck so that, except for the seamlessness of these surfaces, it has all the character of its wood original. The reinterpreted Fish that Cape Cod Shipbuilding calls the Marlin has a slightly larger twenty-three-foot (7m) fiberglass hull modified to carry a modern rig with aluminum spars and permanent backstay. There is also a redesigned deck with fiberglass rounded-front cabin trunk to provide more headroom in the small cabin. Cape Cod also produces a "Cruiser" version on the Marlin hull with an even longer cabin trunk.

The famous 12 ½, still active in racing fleets of the original 12 ½s and Bull's Eyes that were built between 1914 and 1943, has been kept alive in fiberglass by both Cape Cod and Doughdish, Inc., of Marion, Massachusetts. The Cape Cod 12½ is a slight modification of the 1914 original, based on a sister class, the Fishers Island Sound Bull's Eye of 1938, and is given a small fiberglass cabin trunk and a Marconi rig on aluminum spars. Cape Cod also builds an open-cockpit version similar to the 1914 original. The Doughdish is a faithful replica of the 1914 keel daysailer with gaff sailplan, varnished teak seats and trim, spruce spars, and a foam-core fiberglass hull. It is the same capable, beautiful, and roomy little day boat that the wizard of Bristol created more than eighty years ago.

A previous discussion of racing classics includes replica sandbaggers built by Philadelphia's Independence Seaport Museum. These are both replicas and racing classics, and the chapter on racing classics seemed the proper place for them since the few sandbaggers that survive are museum pieces never seen in all their about-to-capsize glory under sail. A British version of the old twenty- to twenty-three-foot (6 to 7m) New York Harbor class of American sandbaggers, with the wonderful name *Fatso the Blagger*, is something else—a sandbagger type reinterpreted and racing a hundred years after the heyday of these extreme sailing machines. Late-twentieth-century sport sailing has seen a revival of such how-much-sail-can-we-put-on-it boats, and *Fatso* is one of them. The hull is the classic skimming dish, now with weighted bulbs at the bottom of keel and rudder. (The original sandbaggers had centerboards.)

Fatso the Blagger recently amazed the rest of the fleet at Cowes Week, the premier series of regattas in England. The Philadelphia sandbagger replicas have done the same at recent Wooden Boat Shows in the United States. Both types oppose the force of the wind on their big sails with weight of crew (and sandbags). As with the tuckups and hikers of a hundred years ago and modern planing dinghies like the *Flying Dutchman*, they do this by hanging out as far as possible on trapeze harnesses with their feet planted on the rail. This doesn't always work, but just before it stops working the boat is going twenty knots (38kph).

Replicas and reinterpretations, as noted, are all about the past. Not all sailors are attracted to the past—in fact, most sailors own modern boats of fiberglass with aluminum spars, Dacron running rigging, and fittings of stainless steel. Sailors have loved the technology since the beginning, from Egyptian sailors learning new knots from the Phoenicians to the New York Yacht Club's 1983 America's Cup sailors learning about winged keels from the Australians. Most sailors like to be modern. But the people who own and design and build the replica classics shown here, and love the real classics shown elsewhere in this book, don't trust modern. They see something tried and true and beautiful in the old boats, and it satisfies them. They may be on to something. Time will tell. Time is on their side.

Note: Sources for plans, patterns, kits, and completed boats can be found at the back of this book.

One of two sandbagger replicas built by Philadelphia's Independence Seaport, *Puffin* has the huge sailplan, long bowsprit, and broad, shallow hull of the celebrated New York Harbor racing machines of the 1880s.

SAILING IS AN OUTDOOR SPORT, PHYSICALLY AND OFTEN MENTAL-
LY DEMANDING, ALWAYS DEPENDENT ON THE WEATHER. UNLIKE
STEAMING ALONG UNDER POWER ABOARD A LUXURY YACHT, WITH
OWNER AND GUESTS ENJOYING THE SCENERY AND PUZZLING OVER THE
CHART WHILE CAPTAIN AND CREW ATTEND TO THE ENGINES
and a timely arrival at the next port of call, sailing a luxury yacht typically involves owner and guests
in navigation, weather prediction, sail-change decisions, and any number of other challenging activi-
ties if they want it to—and usually they do.

Luxury sailing yachts are different from luxury power yachts—a little less luxurious, perhaps,
because most luxury sailboats lack the machinery and electric power for such things as an endless supply of ice cubes and an onboard office with fax and computer access to the world. Because the rig is
in the way, they don't even have boat decks with helicopters. Some, however, have such things as
saunas, deep freezes stocked with coq au vin and lobster Newburg prepared by city restaurants, and
wine cellars, or at least wine bilges. Luxury has many definitions, and for sailors the real luxury may
be the knowledge that a full-comfort sailing yacht can go anywhere on
the world's waters without critical dependence on machinery, electricity, or fuel. And it may be the corollary knowledge, watching Moorea
come over the horizon on a big blue day in the Pacific, that you sailed
here and you can sail anywhere else you please.

Angelique **is a big.
dramatic ketch ninety-
five feet (27.4m) on deck
that takes paying
passengers on Maine-
coast summer tours in
rustic luxury.**

Chapter Seven

JULIET, JESSICA, AND ANGELIQUE

Size and intended purpose tend to define how much and what kind of luxury a sailing yacht will have. Aboard a $22 million modern yacht like *Juliet*, the comforts, the conveniences, and even the indulgences can rival those of the big power megayachts of her size and class. Aboard a yacht like *Jessica*, a deliberate re-creation of the kind of yacht an English lord might have owned a hundred years ago, the luxuries are in keeping with the boat's style—Cuban cigars in seagoing humidors, certainly, but not motorcycles in their own deck-level compartments for shore excursions. And yachts like *When and If*, a big Alden schooner built to sail around the world, and *Angelique*, an even bigger ketch in charter service on the coast of Maine, have deliberately simple comforts and even deliberately simple technologies—the former because, on your own in the South Pacific, a sturdy ship's boat and a lead line will be a better depth sounder approaching badly charted coral islands than the newest electronics, the latter because charter guests on the coast of Maine expect an experience that includes cold fresh air, hot fish chowder, and blisters from handling lines.

Let us begin with *Juliet*, one of a fleet of high-tech, high-style sailing yachts designed and built in the 1980s and 1990s—and one of the great ones. Launched in April 1993 at

OPPOSITE: Luxury yachting in the 1990s is defined by the 143-foot (43.6m) *Juliet*, launched in 1993 by Holland's Royal Huisman Shipyard for an American owner. LEFT: Even the smallest of details are customized on luxury yachts like *Angelique*.

Holland's Royal Huisman Shipyard (at the end of the twentieth century considered to be the world's finest builder of yachts), *Juliet* represents the old luxury of perfect paint and varnish, great sweeps of teak deck, everything below and on deck crafted to please the owner's eye and his or her plans for the vessel, rare woods in furnishings and on bulkheads, other materials like marble and brass, quarters for a crew that includes not only sailors but servants, and voyaging capabilities that encompass the world. Added to this are newer luxuries such as heating and air conditioning throughout this floating mansion, water filters to supply endless fresh water distilled from sea water, electronic navigation and communications capabilities via satellite signal, sails and rigging made from space-age materials and operated with hydraulic machinery, quiet and reliable diesels to substitute for the sails, restaurant-size galley facilities with very deep freezers, and a complement of generators to supply electricity for much of the gear noted above. Let us not forget to mention an essential luxury of most yachts bigger than 100 feet (30.5m)—space for everything, including that most subtle of luxuries, privacy. On a vessel as large as *Juliet*—143 feet (43.5m) on deck, with 29-foot-6-inch (9m) beam—there is space for everything, and everything has its place, with the luxury and reliability of the spaces and the systems all but guaranteed by the engineers and interior designers who planned them.

Some photos in these pages reveal the results of such thoughtful work, along with the superb craftsmanship of the Huisman workforce. Very few objects in this world have the perfection of design, engineering, workmanship, and finish a modern sailing superyacht like this one has. And no objects in this world except for a few yachts like *Juliet* have the comforts and capabilities she and her people will take for granted on some wonderful wild coast. *Juliet* is a traveling mansion. On her maiden voyage she sailed around the world.

Larger than *Juliet*, and no less luxurious, the 203-foot (62m) *Jessica* is both a replica-reinterpretation and a thoroughly modern yacht. She has all the aesthetic characteristics of the big schooner yachts built between 1890 and 1914 for those who could afford them, most of them English or Scottish and frequently men and women with titles. In America the economic nobility that were dubbed robber barons expressed themselves with racing yachts rather than cruising yachts like this big schooner with spoon bow, tall rig with double square topsails, three jibs, a long bowsprit, teak deckhouses inboard from the decks for plenty of sail-handling room, quarters for thirteen crew, and truly luxurious accommodations for the owner's party. Only a few of the great Edwardian yachts have survived, and *Jessica* brings back their style, their craftsmanship, their luxury, and indeed their aura.

This superlative yacht was built of steel by a Spanish shipyard and launched in 1984 for an Argentinian businessman whose interests include industrial construction and shipbuilding. *Jessica*, despite a very accurate replication of the hull, deck structures, rig, and even the interior style of a yacht from a hundred years ago, is state-of-the-art, with satellite navigation and communications gear, all the hot-shower and cold-drinks capabilities of an engine-powered superyacht of her size, big diesels to supplement and substitute

for her considerable sail power, and diesel generators to supply her electrical needs. *Jessica* can go any-

where on the waters of the world and feel like the Plaza Hotel in the process.

Another striking replica-reinterpretation is *Angelique*, a gaff-rigged ketch 95 feet (29m) on

deck and 130 feet (39.6m) from the end of her mizzen boom to the tip of her long bowsprit.

Designed along the lines of England's legendary Brixham trawlers, although twice as large, and given

a nineteenth-century sailplan with brick red sails and lots of lines to pull and adjust, *Angelique* earns

her living in the charter fleet on the coast of Maine. Her style and her luxuries are rustic—guest cab-

ins reminiscent of a cottage on a lake, gourmet meals and regional specialties like New England

chowders coming out of her deckhouse galley, the islands of the Maine coast for scenery, and wildlife

(including whales) for company. Another luxury she offers the sedentary city dwellers among her

guests—something that was anything but luxury to sailing-vessel hands a century ago—is the satis-

fying workout of hauling on lines and adjusting the set of some very big sails.

Launched in 1984 as *Jessica*, and now under new ownership with a new name, *Adix*, this 203-foot (61.9m) schooner with spoon bow and bowsprit, varnished wood deckhouses, and gaff sailplan is a re-creation of the great cruising yachts of the Edwardian era.

BELLE AVENTURE, ALTAIR, AND WHEN AND IF

Every September in St. Tropez, Europe's classic sailing yachts, along with some of the big new racing machines, gather for La Nioulargue—a race meeting, a free-form party, an antique-boat show, a gathering of the faithful. In the 1970s, 1980s, and 1990s many of Europe's great old yachts were given careful and very expensive restorations, and La Nioulargue is where they are shown off after a summer in the Med.

Two of the great classic luxury yachts that may be in attendance are *Belle Aventure* and *Altair*, both built in Scotland by the legendary Fife family of yacht designers and builders. These are both big cruising yachts in the Fife tradition of sweeping lines and perfect workmanship on deck and below. *Belle Aventure*, a 95-foot (29m) ketch with tall Marconi sailplan, was built in 1929 for a Scottish owner. *Altair*, a 107-foot (32.5m) gaff-rigged schooner, was launched in 1931 for another Scottish owner who hoped to cruise the South Seas. Both boats passed through a succession of situations until the 1970s, when they were given thorough restorations by new owners who had caught the old-boat fervor that began in that decade when great old vessels, from big yachts to small launches, were suddenly missed on the waterfront and just as suddenly valued again and revived. *Altair*'s baronial below-decks spaces include a wood-paneled saloon with an electric fireplace. *Belle Aventure*, perfectly restored and now perfectly kept, has been described as "by any standard one of the world's most beautiful, flawlessly maintained yachts." Both of these classic Fife creations represent a prewar yachting luxury that returned in the 1990s with sailing megayachts like *Juliet*.

The U.S. version of cruising luxury in the 1930s, with only a few exceptions, was a big, capable, deep-draft Alden schooner in which to sail over the horizon and sample the legendary adventures of coconut land. This was what the equally legendary George S. Patton had in mind when he was still a U.S. Army colonel in 1938. That year this sixty-three-foot-five-inch (19.3m), eighty-five-thousand-pound (38.5t) deep-water schooner was built for Patton in Maine as Alden design number 669 and given the name *When and If*. Patton saw World War II in his future and planned to sail her around the world when and if the world and its troubles gave him the opportunity. The world didn't; the great Patton died in an auto accident in Europe in 1945. *When and If* passed through several owners, deteriorating all the time, until the 1990s, when she was acquired by yacht builder Nat Benjamin and

PREVIOUS PAGES: **One of the great sailing luxury yachts, the 214-foot (65.2m) schooner** *Creole* **was built for an American yachtsman who cruised and raced frequently in Europe. She is now owned by the Gucci family.**

OPPOSITE: **A big gaff-rigged schooner launched in 1931 by Scotland's Fife yard.** *Altair* **defines prewar yachting luxury in size, power, and such comforts as a fireplace in her wood-paneled saloon.**

yachting book editor Jim Mairs. After a thorough restoration, she now sails in schooner races and antique-yacht gatherings on the U.S. East Coast, and cruises New England in the summer. She's a classic John Alden South Seas dreamboat, a simple and capable vessel intended for an anchorage in a coral lagoon.

NEWER LUXURY VESSELS

Some newer members of this go-anywhere-in-luxury fleet include production yachts like the Hinckley 70 and the Little Harbor 60, and custom-built yachts like the eighty-foot (24.3m) steel ketch *Oz*. In the 1950s, when Little Harbor's Ted Hood was a young sailmaker in Marblehead, Massachusetts, and Henry Hinckley was building stock wooden yachts up in Maine and experimenting with something called fiberglass, most of the world's sailing yachts were custom-designed and custom-built. Only a few of them were

bigger than fifty feet (15.2m), and the number of sailing-yacht owners was relatively small compared with the numbers today. During the 1960s there occurred an explosion of both an interest in sailing that has never been properly explained and fiberglass production-line boatbuilding, which was certainly part of the explanation. Hinckley and Hood would have snickered in the 1950s at the notion of anything as grand as a sailing industry. But since the 1960s there has truly been a sailing industry, and it now includes impressive fiberglass production yachts like Hood's Little Harbor 60 and the Hinckley family's seventy-footer (21.3m). This sailing industry serves a large sailing constituency all over the world. At the upper level of this constituency are people who want, and are able to afford, yachts of great luxury, capability, and safety, not to mention cruising or racing performance and suitability for that coral lagoon where all the world's cruising yachts set their anchors in the dreams of their owners.

Both the Hinckley 70 and the Little Harbor 60 are suitable coconut-land cruisers, keel-centerboard designs with deep draft for ocean passages and shallower draft when their centerboards are raised. The Hinckley 70 has a seventy-foot-three-inch(21.4m) overall length, a seventeen-foot-six-inch (5.3m) beam, and a ninety-thousand-pound (40.8t) displacement, while the Little Harbor 60 has a sixty-one-foot-three-inch (18.6m) overall length, a sixteen-foot-six-inch (5m) beam, and a seventy-eight-thousand-pound (35.3t) displacement. These are big envelopes in which to package luxury quarters for owner, guests, and crew, along with mechanical and electronic equipment that ranges from air conditioning to gear for satellite communication, weather forecast, and navigation. The Hinckley 70's basic arrangement plan provides quarters for an owner's party of eight and a crew of two. This is a semicustom yacht with other below-decks arrangements possible. There are four options in deck configurations for this big cruising sloop, including one with a deckhouse. The Little Harbor 60 provides quarters for two crew and an owner's party of six to eight.

OPPOSITE: A big, go-anywhere steel ketch built in New Zealand, the eighty-foot (24.4m) *Oz* has served several cruising owners, as well as a movie crew, since she was launched in 1982. ABOVE: Among the new luxury yachts from semicustom boatbuilders is the Hinckley 70, built in several versions with quarters for an owner's party of eight and a professional crew of two.

More traditional-looking than these two sleek production yachts, the eighty-foot (24.3m) steel ketch *Oz* was custom-built in New Zealand and equipped by a film-producer owner with specialized gear for scuba diving and film work. The working gear ranges from large electrical capacity in diesel generators and banks of batteries to a hot tub built into the afterdeck—a place where divers warm up after cold-water work. Down below, among other comforts and conveniences for a crew of three and an owner's party of as many as a dozen, is a sauna. All of *Oz*'s spaces, including an immaculate engine room, are fitted with built-ins and trim of satin-varnished wood, and most of them have the warmth of wood on bulkheads.

THE GREAT J-BOATS

Built for racing during the 1930s, the legendary J-boats that have survived are now fitted out as cruising yachts, and necessarily cruising yachts of great luxury. *Shamrock V* was launched in 1930 as the first of the Js and the last of Sir Thomas Lipton's British challengers for the America's Cup. *Endeavour*, the first of two J-class yachts of that name built for England's T.O.M. Sopwith, challenged for the America's Cup in 1934 and nearly won it. There were ten yachts built to the J-class rule between 1929 and 1938, and *Shamrock V* and *Endeavour* are among the three survivors, along with a restored English J named *Velsheda*. The Js were strictly racing machines in their heyday, and by the time J-class racing ended at the beginning of World War II the other seven were gone, broken up and sold for the scrap value of their metal.

Contemporary luxury yachts combine sophisticated systems and gear, quarters as fully luxurious as the great yachts of the past, and low-maintenance fiberglass hulls. This is the Little Harbor 60, designed and built by Ted Hood.

Under Italian ownership in the 1970s, *Shamrock V* was given a thorough refit and restoration that included sumptuous quarters for owner and guests, comfortable crew spaces forward, and a deckhouse full of electronics. *Shamrock V* has since been owned by the Lipton Tea Company, the Museum of Yachting in Newport, Rhode Island, and now by Elizabeth Meyer's International Yacht Restoration School in Newport.

Elizabeth Meyer could be said to be in the J-boat business. She also owns *Endeavour*, and both of these great yachts are maintained and chartered by her company in Newport, J-Class Management. *Endeavour* was a steel hulk in the mud of the Medina River on England's Isle of Wight when a brave British couple acquired her and began a restoration that was, in the beginning, more of a resuscitation. They and their friends got her floating again and made essential structural repairs before Elizabeth Meyer bought her and began a $10 million project to bring her back to her former glory.

As the photo above shows, *Endeavour* is now an extraordinary cruising yacht, combining the rakishness and power of a J-boat's bladelike hull and tall sailplan with below-decks accommodations made almost entirely from select cherrywood. The deck is 130 feet (39.6m) of carefully laid raw teak, and on-deck structures are varnished teak. The restoration's steelwork was done in England; the rest of this unprecedented rebuilding of a great yacht was done by Holland's Royal Huisman Shipyard, the builder of *Juliet*, discussed previously.

Luxury sailing yachts like *Juliet* and *Endeavour* are nothing less than floating mansions, and if their spaces are smaller than the vast drawing rooms and long galleries of great houses, they are no less luxurious. The really big space a sailing yacht can boast extends to the horizon, and it changes whenever a lucky owner and his or her crew decides to sail on. Then the space extends to the whole watery world.

Note: Sources for plans, patterns, kits, and completed boats can be found at the back of this book.

OPPOSITE: Another surviving J-class yacht, Sir Thomas Lipton's *Shamrock V* challenged for the America's Cup in 1930, and is now a part of the fleet of the International Yacht Restoration School. ABOVE: Built in 1934 by England's T.O.M. Sopwith to challenge for the America's Cup. *Endeavour* was restored in the mid-1980s by Elizabeth Meyer of Newport. Rhode Island. FOLLOWING PAGES: *Adix* combines old-world luxury with state-of-the-art technology, allowing her wealthy owners to travel the world in comfort and style.

UNITED STATES

John G. Alden
Yacht Design and Yacht
Brokerage
89 Commercial Wharf
Boston, MA 02110

Angelique
Yankee Packet Company
Box 736
Camden, ME 04843-0736

John Atkin
Boat and Yacht Design
Box 3005
Noroton, CT 06820

Bill of Rights
VisionQuest
Box 447
Exton, PA 19341

Philip C. Bolger
Boat Designer
29 Ferry Street
Gloucester, MA 01930

Bridges Point Boat Yard
Box 342
Brooklin, ME 04616

Californian
The Nautical Heritage
Society
24532 Del Prado
Dana Point, CA 92629

Cape Cod Shipbuilding
7 Narrows Road
Wareham, MA 02571
The Catboat Association
c/o Max Fife
Box 427
Stockton Springs, ME 04941

The Chesapeake Bay Sailing
Log Canoe Association
c/o Miles River Yacht Club
Box 158
St. Michaels, MD 21663

Clearwater
Hudson River Sloop
Clearwater
112 Market Street
Poughkeepsie, NY 12601-
4095

The Concordia Company
Box P-203
South Dartmouth, MA 02748

Doughdish, Inc.
380 Wareham Road
Marion, MA 02738

Dyer Dinghies
The Anchorage
57 Miller Street
Warren, RI 02885

Edey & Duff
128 Aucoot Road
Mattapoisett, MA 02739

Eel plans
See The WoodenBoat Store

Egret plans
See The WoodenBoat Store

Epifanes North America
58 Fore Street
Portland, ME 04101

The Friendship Sloop Society
Box 159
Friendship, ME 04547

Glen-L Marine Designs
9152 Rosecrans Avenue
Bellflower, CA 90706

H-28 plans
See L. Francis Herreshoff
Plans

Harvey Gamage
Schooner *Harvey Gamage*
Foundation
Box 60
Francestown, NH 03043

The Hinckley Company
130 Shore Road
Southwest Harbor, ME 04679

Independence Seaport
Museum
Penn's Landing
211 South Columbus
Boulevard
at Walnut Street
Philadelphia, PA 19106

International Yacht
Restoration School
449 Thames Street
Newport, RI 02840

Itatae plans
See William Garden

J-Class Management
28 Church Street
Newport, RI 02840

Lady Maryland
Living Classrooms
Foundation
The Lighthouse, Pier V
717 Eastern Avenue
Baltimore, MD 21202

L. Francis Herreshoff Plans
Elizabeth Vaughn
620 Galland Street
Petaluma, CA 94952

Little Harbor Yachts
1 Little Harbor Landing
Portsmouth, RI 02871

M. Rosenblatt & Son, Inc.
Naval Architects
350 Broadway
New York, NY 10013

Marshall Marine
Box P-266
South Dartmouth, MA 02748

Middleton Marine
Box 45
LaCrosse, FL 32658

Mystic Seaport Museum
Publications
75 Greenmanville Avenue
Mystic, CT 06355

Mystic Seaport Museum
Watercraft Plans
75 Greenmanville Avenue
Mystic, CT 06355

Nereia plans
See L. Francis Herreshoff
Plans

Newman Marine
254 Main Street
Southwest Harbor, ME 04679

Noank Marine Service
Beebe Cove Marina
55 Spicer Avenue
Groton, CT 06340
or Box 9492
Noank, CT 06340

Pride of Baltimore
Pride of Baltimore, Inc.
401 East Pratt Street
Baltimore, MD 21202

Rumery's Boat Yard
109 Cleaves Street
Biddeford, ME 04005

Sanford Boat Works
Lower Pleasant Street
Nantucket, MA 02554

The Sharpie Association
c/o Peter Vermilya
Mystic Seaport Museum
75 Greenmanville Avenue
Mystic, CT 06355

Spirit of Massachusetts
197 Eighth Street
Charlestown Navy Yard
Boston, MA 02129

Tahiti Ketch plans
Helen Hanna Brown
30 Winchester Road #83
Goleta, CA 93117

The Traditional Small Craft
Association
P.O. Box 350
Mystic, CT 06355

The United States Sailing
Association
Box 1260
15 Maritime Drive
Portsmouth, RI 02871

Van Dam Wood Craft
970 East Division Street
Boyne City, MI 49712

Joel White
Boat Designer and
Boatbuilder
Brooklin Boatyard
Center Harbor Road
Brooklin, ME 04616

WoodenBoat
Naskeag Road
Brooklin, ME 04616

The WoodenBoat Store
Box 78
Brooklin, ME 04616

CANADA
The Dory Shop
Box 1678
Lunenburg, NS B0J 2C0

William Garden
Boat and Yacht Designer
Box 2371
Sidney, British Columbia
V8L 3Y3

Ludlow Boatworks
RR#4 Becketts Landing
Kemptville, ON K0G 1J0

The Tender Craft Boat Shop,
Inc.
284 Brock Avenue
Toronto, ON M6K 2M4

UNITED KINGDOM
Classic Boat
Link House
Dingwall Avenue
Croydon, Surrey CR9 2TA
England

Cornish Crabbers Ltd
Rock, Wadebridge
Cornwall PL27 6PH
England

Dartington Boatworks
Steverton Bridge Mill
Totnes, Devon TQ9 6AH
England

Nigel Irens Design
Staverton Bridge Mill
Totnes, Devon TQ9 6AH
England

Iain Oughtred
Boat Designer
Gorton House Cottage
Lasswade, Edinburgh EH18
1EH
Scotland

FRANCE
Chasse-Marée
Abri du Marin
B.P. 159
29177 Douarnenez Cedex

THE NETHERLANDS
The Royal Huisman Shipyard
8325ZG Vollenhove

FINLAND
Nauticat Yachts
Siltala Yachts Oy
Turku

AUSTRALIA
The Wooden Boatshop
192 Hotham Road
Sorrento 3943

Drascombe Boats
Australia Pty Ltd.
RMB 209
Lemon Tree Passage Road
Salt Ash, NSW 2318

Acorn dinghies, 56–57
Adix, 113, *113*
Alden schooner, 72
Alerion, replicas of, 104–106, *105*
Altair, 116, *117*
America, 28, 104
America's Cup, 82
Ancient world, sailing in, 15–18
Angelique, *108*, 109–110, *110*, 113
Aquidneck, 63
Arabs, and early sailing, 19, *20*, 22
Atlantic class, 86, *88*, 89

Baltimore clippers, 40
Baltimore schooners, 40, *40*
Beachcomber-Alpha, 49
Beetle Cat, 50, *51*
Belle Aventure, 116
Bill of Rights, 42, *42*, 43
Block Island cowhorns, *36*, 38
Bluebottle, 88
Breck Marshall, *38*
Brigantines, *33*
Burma, 74, 75

Californian, 42
Canoes, sailing, *31*, 58
    log, 37, *39*, 85, *85*
    Polynesian, 20
Canoe yawls, 57–58, *58*
Cape Cod catboat, *38*
    reinterpretations, 97–98, *102–103*
Carracks, *23*
Catamarans, 20
Catboats, 34, 37–38, *48*, 50, *50–51*, 66, 74–75
    Cape Cod, *38*, 97–98, *102–103*
Cat-ketch, *36*, 37
Catspaw dinghy, 56–57, *57*
Character boats, 35
Chebacco 20, 97–98, *99*
Chesapeake Bay
    log canoes, 37, *39*, 85, *85*
    Pungy schooners, 40–42
China, sailing in, 21–22, *22*
Clearwater, 40, *41*
Clippers, 40, 70
Clipper-style fishing schooners, 42
Concordias, 73, *73*

Cornish Crabber 24, 98–100, *101*
Cornish Cutter 24, 98–100
Creole, 13, *114–115*, 116
Cruising, 64–66
Cruising boats, 66–76
Cruising-racing yachts, 73–74, *73*
    Cutters, *30*, 34, 42
Cutter yachts, *31*, *33*

Day boats, 46–61
Delaware Duckers, 37
Dinghies, 38, 52, 55–57, *55*, 96, *97*
Dorade, 89–90, *91*
Dories, 38, 48–49
Dory skiffs, 48–49, *49*
Doughdish, 106
Dragon one-design class, 86
Dyer sailing dinghies, 55–57

Eel canoe yawl, 58, *58*
Egret, 60
Endeavour, 121, 123, *123*
Europe, sailing history in, 23–27, 32

Fatso the Blagger, 106
Fiberglass boats, 52–54, 104–106
Fife cutter, 30
Fish class, replicas of, 106
Fishing boats, reinterpretations, 98–100, 102
Flatiron skiffs, 50
Friendship sloops, 102

Galleons, 26
Gleam, *84*, 85
Glory Anna, 36
Greek ships, 16, *17*
Grimalkin, 58–60, *59*

Harvey Gamage, 42
Herreshoff S-boats, *82*, 83
Hinckley 70, 118–119, *119*
Hinckley Sou'wester 42, 72, *72*, 73–74
Hokule'a, *14*, 15
H-28s, 67, 70

International 14, 86–87
International One Design (IOD)
    class, 86, *86*, 88

International Rule, 80–82, 84
Islander, 76
Itatae, 66

J-class yachts, 82, 121–123
Jessica, 110, 112–113, *113*
Joe Lane, Californian, 42
Juliet, 110–112, *111*
Junks, *22*

Ketches, 32, *108*
Kit-boats, 95–96

Lady Maryland, 40–42
Lateen sail, 19–20, *20–21*
Liberdade, 63
Lightning one-design class, 58
Little Harbor 60, 118–119, *120*, 121
Log canoes, 37, *39*, 85, *85*
Longships, Viking, 23–24, *25*
Luxury yachts, 109–123

Malabar II, 71, *71*, 72–73
Marblehead dory skiff, 49, *49*
Marlin, 52, 54, 106
Marshall 22, *102–103*
Matthew, replica, 24, 25
Motorsailers, *74*, 75

Nauticats, 75
Navigation, early, 20–21, 25
Nereia, 70
New York, *31*, *31*, 35–37, *37*

Ocean sailing, 63–64. *See also*
    Cruising; Racing, ocean
One-design classes, 80, 86–88
Oriole II, 88–89, *89*
Oz, 118, *118*, 121

Patrician, 58–61, *60–61*
Piccolo sailing canoe, 58
Polynesia, 20–21
Pride of Baltimore, 40, *40*
Puffin, 107
Pungy schooners, 40–42

Racing, 35–37, 78–80
    ocean, 80, 89–90
    one-design, 80–88

Racing boats, 49, 54–55, 79–90
    classification rules, 80–82
    oceangoing, 73–74, 80
    from workboats, 35, 37–40, *39*
Racing scows, 85
Recreational sailboats, 34–40. *See also* Day boats; Yachts
Reinterpretations/Replicas, 40–44, 93–107
Roman ships, *18*, 19
Rosa II, *70*, 71
Roxane, 98, *99*

Sailing, 8–12
    early history of, 15–27
    nineteenth-century, 29–44
Sailing vessels. *See also specific types*
    early, 15–18, *17*, 22, *22*, 27
    nineteenth-century, 29–44
    small, 31, 67. *See also* Day boats
    twentieth-century romance
        with, 31
Sails, 18–22, 27, 32. *See also*
    Square sails
Sakonnet 23, 52–54, *54*
Sallee Rover sloop, 66, 76
Sandbaggers, *31*, 35, 84, 107, *107*
S-boats, *See* Herreshoff S-boats
Schooners, 29, 32, 35, *65*
    Alden, 72
    Baltimore, 40, *40*
    coasting, 42, *42*
    cruising, *65*, 66, 71, *71*
    Pungy, 40
    replicas, 40–43, *40–43*
    topsail, *33*, 42
Scow, racing, 85
Shamrock V, 121, *123*
Sharpies, *34*, 35, 38
Sharpie skiffs, 38
Shellback dinghies, 56–57, *57*, 96, *97*
6-meter boats, 83–84
Skiffs, 38, 50–52
    dory, 48–49, *49*
Skipjacks, 38
Sloops, 32–35, 37–38, 66, *78*
    Friendship, 102
    Sallee Rover, 66, 76
Smacks, 38
Spirit of Massachusetts, 42, *43*

Spray, 75–76
Spritsail, 19
Square sails, 16, 19, 21–22, 27
Star, 86, *86*
Steam vessels, 29
Stone Horse, 100–101, *100*,
Sydney 18s, 85

Tacking, 19
Tancook Whalers, 38
30-square-meter class, 88
Ticonderoga, 66, *67*, 70
Topsail schooner, *33*
12-meter yachts, 82, 84, *84*

Universal Rule, 80–82
U.S. revenue cutters, 42

Velsheda, 121
Victura, 80
Vikings, 23–25

Western Skiff, 96, *96*, 97
When and If, 110, 116–118
Whitehall boats, 38
Whitehawk, *68–69*, 70
Wianno Seniors, 80, *81*
Wooden boats, care of, 52
Workboats, 38–40
    modern boats based on, 98–100, 102–104
    racing boats based on, 38–40
    yachts based on, 34–35

Yachting, history of, 29, 31, 34–37
Yachts, 31, 109–123. *See also*
    Cruising boats; Racing boats
    clipper, 70
    cruising-racing, 73–74, *73*
    cutter, 31, 33
    tenders, 55
    workboat-style, 35
Yawls, 57–58, *58*, 66, 76

Zulu, *62*, 63, 76, *76*